Also available at all good book stores

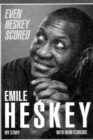

9781785315008

9781785313875

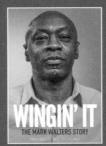

9781785314407

9781785315992

9781785313967

9781909626584

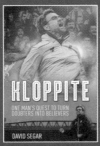

9781785313066

9781785311932

9781785314490

LIVERPOOL MINUTE BY MINUTE

LIVERPOOL
MINUTE
BY MINUTE

Covering More Than 500 Goals,
Penalties, Red Cards and
Other Intriguing Facts

DAVID JACKSON

First published by Pitch Publishing, 2020

Pitch Publishing
A2 Yeoman Gate
Yeoman Way
Worthing
Sussex
BN13 3QZ
www.pitchpublishing.co.uk
info@pitchpublishing.co.uk

A CIP catalogue record is available for this book
from the British Library.

ISBN 978 1 78531 629 6

Typesetting and origination by Pitch Publishing
Printed and bound in India by Replika Press Pvt. Ltd.

Contents

Acknowledgements. 9

Foreword by Paul Walsh 11

Introduction 13

1st Minute 15

2nd Minute 17

3rd Minute 19

4th Minute 21

5th Minute 24

6th Minute 25

7th Minute 27

8th Minute 29

9th Minute 31

10th Minute 33

11th Minute 35

12th Minute 38

13th Minute 40

14th Minute 43

15th Minute 44

16th Minute 47

17th Minute 50

18th Minute 52

19th Minute 54

20th Minute 57

21st Minute. 60

22nd Minute 63

23rd Minute 65

24th Minute 67

25th Minute 69
26th Minute 71
27th Minute 73
28th Minute 74
29th Minute 77
30th Minute 80
31st Minute. 82
32nd Minute 84
33rd Minute 87
34th Minute 89
35th Minute 92
36th Minute 95
37th Minute 97
38th Minute 99
39th Minute 101
40th Minute 103
41st Minute. 105
42nd Minute 107
43rd Minute 109
44th Minute 111
45th Minute 114
45+1 Minute 116
45+2 Minutes. 117
45+3 Minutes. 118
46th Minute 119
47th Minute 121
48th Minute 124
49th Minute 125
50th Minute 127
51st Minute. 129
52nd Minute 130
53rd Minute 133
54th Minute 135

55th Minute 137
56th Minute 140
57th Minute 144
58th Minute 147
59th Minute 149
60th Minute 151
61st Minute 155
62nd Minute 158
63rd Minute 160
64th Minute 163
65th Minute 166
66th Minute 168
67th Minute 169
68th Minute 170
69th Minute 172
70th Minute 174
71st Minute 176
72nd Minute 177
73rd Minute 178
74th Minute 180
75th Minute 182
76th Minute 185
77th Minute 188
78th Minute 190
79th Minute 192
80th Minute 195
81st Minute 198
82nd Minute 201
83rd Minute 204
84th Minute 206
85th Minute 208
86th Minute 211
87th Minute 213

88th Minute 216
89th Minute 220
90th Minute 223
90+1 Minute 227
92nd Minute 229
90+2 Minutes. 230
90+3 Minutes. 231
93rd Minute 232
90+4 Minutes. 233
90+5 Minutes. 235
95th Minute 237
90+6 Minutes. 238
98th Minute 239
99th Minute 240
103rd Minute. 241
104th Minute. 242
107th Minute. 243
108th Minute. 244
109th Minute. 245
111th Minute. 246
117th Minute. 247
118th Minute. 248
119th Minute. 249
Penalty Shoot-outs 250

For Phil and Joseph Adams #YNWA

Acknowledgements

Liverpool: Minute by Minute was a hard book to research, but thanks to certain resource outlets, it was made a lot easier. The goal times are from various places: BBC match reports, Sky Sports games, *Match of the Day*, the *Liverpool Echo* (and countless newspaper clippings), plus Liverpool FC's official website. A huge thanks goes to the dedicated duo that are Arnie Baldursson and Gudmundur Magnusson – the Icelandic Reds behind the magnificent *LFC History* (lfchistory.net) – and their tireless work in creating an accessible database that this book would have been so much harder to write without. Thanks guys!

Finally, to Paul and Jane – the tireless siblings who mastermind Pitch Publishing – for green-lighting this project. It's been on Paul's radar for three or four years and finally we have an end result ...

Foreword by Paul Walsh

As a footballer, you have to make every single minute count.

During your playing days, you don't think that way because you always have the next game coming along and then the one after that – so if it doesn't happen for you in one match, maybe it will in the one coming up.

In hindsight, every minute matters.

For me, my first game at Anfield will be forever etched into my memory.

In many ways, I am lucky because there is a permanent record in the history books of my first few seconds as a Liverpool player at Anfield.

In short, it was a dream start and the beginning of an exhilarating period of my career.

My mum and dad came up for my home debut and, ironically, we were playing the side my dad had followed all his life, West Ham. It was August 1984 and it was exhilarating to see the Kop full and hear the noise they generated in the flesh and I'd like to think I rose to the occasion.

We had just kicked off when Ronnie Whelan intercepted a pass and put me through on goal and I was never going to pass up that opportunity. We'd played just 14 seconds and I'd scored inside the first minute of my home debut. It really doesn't get any better than that.

I made a goal for John Wark later in a game we went on to win 3-0 – a goal and an assist was close to the start I'd dreamed of.

At the other end of the spectrum, the latest goal I scored during my time with Liverpool was a 119th-minute equaliser against Manchester United in an FA Cup semi-final at Goodison Park, so I probably came as close as anyone has got to scoring one of the earliest and latest goals for the Reds.

I thoroughly enjoyed my time at Anfield and with a bit more luck and a few less injuries, I think things would have been different for me. Of the 112 games I played, I scored 37 goals – I'd be lying if I said I remembered every minute they were scored in, but this book recounts a few of them and pretty much every major goal scored for Liverpool since the year dot.

I feel honoured that I can say I played my part in the history of this football club and can assure you of one thing – I loved every minute of it.

Introduction

Liverpool have an extraordinary history. From the very early successes of the 1900s, to the glorious Bill Shankly era of the 1960s and early 1970s, and then into the trophy-laden Bob Paisley years. Champions of England, then Europe, before dominating the domestic landscape for more than 20 years. Then there was the Miracle of Istanbul and so many near misses in the Premier League up until Jürgen Klopp's mesmerising team of today.

All the finals at home and abroad and all the goals that meant so much, stretching back to the club's formation in 1892 to the title-chasing side of 2019/20. *Liverpool: Minute by Minute* is the story of a club who have ridden a rollercoaster of emotions, happy and sad, incredible and tragic.

Every goal that mattered and the minute it was scored in, plus the date and description of how it ended up in the onion bag, not to mention sending-offs and other moments that are forever etched in the psyche of Liverpool supporters.

Now, sit back and enjoy as we turn on the clock and move minute by minute through this wonderful club's playing history ... and beyond.

1

16 February 1938

Jack Balmer scores Liverpool's fastest league goal as the Reds get the perfect start in the Merseyside derby at Goodison Park. Though reports vary, the officially recorded time is just ten seconds, as T.G. Jones's poor clearance falls to Balmer, who makes no mistake to put Liverpool 1-0 up. Though the Toffees level just seven minutes later, two late John Shafto goals complete a much-needed 3-1 win for the Reds.

27 August 1984

Paul Walsh makes an incredible start to life as a Liverpool player by scoring after just 14 seconds of his home debut against West Ham United. The diminutive striker, signed for £700,000 from Luton Town, will score 37 goals in 112 games for the Reds, though injuries affect his time at Anfield. The Reds go on to win the game against the Hammers 3-0.

8 May 1979

Liverpool make a dream start against Aston Villa as Bob Paisley's side look for the win that will clinch an 11th top-flight title. With only 47 seconds on the clock, Terry McDermott crosses in to find full-back Alan Kennedy, who makes no mistake from close range. The Reds go on to win 3-0 and the victory ensures second-placed West Brom can't catch Bob Paisley's side, who also post a record number of points – 68 – during the two-points-for-a-win era.

14 December 1996

Robbie Fowler moves on to 99 goals for Liverpool as he puts the Reds ahead against Middlesbrough after just 29 seconds at Anfield. It leaves the youngster just one shy of reaching a century in record time – and he won't have to wait long to achieve that feat ...

1 November 1997

Robbie Fowler gives Liverpool the perfect start at the Reebok Stadium against Bolton Wanderers. With just one win from their opening six Premier League away games, the Reds look set to go on to claim three points, but will be pegged back by a late Wanderers leveller.

26 April 2019

Naby Keita scores Liverpool's fastest ever Premier League goal. Hosting Huddersfield Town at Anfield, the visitors kick off and play the ball back to their goalkeeper, who in turn, plays a pass to a team-mate just outside the box. But Keita is quick to dispossess him and play it to Mo Salah, who returns the ball to Keita just inside the box, and he hits a low shot across the keeper and into the far corner with just 15 seconds on the clock.

2

16 March 1977

Trailing 1-0 on aggregate in the European Cup third round, Liverpool look to use the red-hot Anfield atmosphere to rattle the French champions – and with only two minutes played, Kevin Keegan scores a goal that sends the 55,043 crowd wild. After receiving a short corner from Steve Heighway, Keegan sends in a deep cross that the St Etienne keeper misjudges, and the ball sails over his head and into the back of the net. It was almost certainly a cross, but the Liverpool fans don't care.

15 March 1997

Robbie Fowler gets Liverpool off to the perfect start away to Nottingham Forest. Jamie Redknapp's crossfield pass to Jason McAteer sees the Reds No. 4 get past one challenge before whipping a low ball into the box, where Fowler makes no mistake.

21 November 1998

Liverpool get off to a great start at Villa Park, as Paul Ince rises highest to head a free kick past Michael Oakes to put the Reds 1-0 up against Aston Villa with only a couple of minutes on the clock.

12 August 2001

Gary McAllister gives Liverpool the perfect start in the 2001 FA Charity Shield clash with Manchester United at the Millennium Stadium in Cardiff. Danny Murphy is fouled in the box and from the resulting penalty, McAllister sends Fabien Barthez the wrong way to make it 1-0.

1 June 2019

Mo Salah emphatically thumps home the opening goal of the 2018/19 Champions League Final from the penalty spot after Sadio Mané's cross had been handballed by Moussa Sissoko. After the disappointment of 12 months earlier, it is the perfect start to the final and one Tottenham won't recover from.

3

17 August 1964

Liverpool play their first ever game in European competition, beginning in the European Cup preliminary round away to Icelandic minnows Knattspyrnufélag Reykjavíkur. The Reds take to European competition like the proverbial ducks to water, and Gordon Wallace has the honour of scoring Liverpool's first European goal, after fine work from Roger Hunt sets up the young Scot on the edge of the six-yard box, and his mishit shot beats the keeper and opens the scoring with just 180 seconds of the game played. It looked like the Reds might enjoy playing in Europe ...

22 January 1966

Liverpool host Chelsea in the FA Cup third round at Anfield, looking to defend the trophy they'd won against Leeds United the previous season. The Reds couldn't ask for a better start as Peter Thompson weaves past one challenge on the left before his cross finds the head of Ian St John, and his knock-down is emphatically thumped home by Roger Hunt from close range. The visitors, playing some excellent football, would come back to win the tie 2-1.

17 September 1974

When Alec Lindsay puts Liverpool ahead against Strømsgodset from the penalty spot in the European Cup

Winners' Cup first round first leg at Anfield, few could predict what would follow, as the Reds go on to put the Norwegians to the sword in an 11-0 romp.

3 May 1980

David Johnson gets Liverpool off to the perfect start as he scores after just three minutes against Aston Villa at Anfield. It's the Reds striker's 26th goal of the campaign and it sets up a 4-1 victory that confirms a 12th top-flight title triumph for Bob Paisley's side.

3 April 1996

Robbie Fowler scores the first of what will be a seven-goal thriller against Newcastle United. Stan Collymore does well on the left of the Magpies box and hooks a cross into the six-yard box, where Fowler nods home from close range to get the Reds off to the perfect start against Kevin Keegan's side.

22 February 2015

Liverpool strike first at St Mary's with a wonder-strike from Philippe Coutinho. The Brazilian collects the ball midway inside the Saints half, then looks up and fires a 30-yard shot that hits the underside of the crossbar before bouncing down and high up into the roof of the net to put the Reds 1-0 up.

4

4 May 1965

In front of a capacity Anfield crowd, Roger Hunt puts Liverpool ahead after just four minutes against Inter Milan in the European Cup semi-final first leg. Hunt sweeps home Ian Callaghan's low cross from the right to give Bill Shankly's side the perfect start.

20 May 1989

In the second all-Merseyside FA Cup Final in three years, the Reds strike first as Steve McMahon leads a counter-attack, before squaring to the edge of the box for John Aldridge to fire a shot high and powerfully past Neville Southall to give Liverpool the perfect start.

6 November 1991

Trailing 2-0 on aggregate to Auxerre in the UEFA Cup second round, the Reds make the perfect start in the second leg at Anfield after Steve McManaman is fouled in the box and Jan Mølby coolly converts the spot kick to halve the deficit.

16 May 2001

Markus Babbel puts Liverpool ahead in the UEFA Cup Final against Alavés at the Westfalenstadion in Dortmund. After being awarded a free kick on the right of the Alavés box, Gary McAllister whips in a cross that Babbel rises to and heads the Reds in front from close range.

3 May 2005

Luis Garcia scores a controversial goal to give Liverpool a dream start in the Champions League semi-final second leg. Having drawn the first leg 0-0 with Chelsea at Stamford Bridge, the Reds are looking to get an early goal and a lead to defend. As Milan Baros chases Steven Gerrard's clever flick into the box, Petr Cech manages to stop the first shot, but Garcia follows up to knock the loose ball towards the empty net and despite William Gallas's attempt to clear it, it is judged to have marginally crossed the line and a goal is awarded. It proves to be the only goal of either leg, with the Reds booking a place in the final thanks to a 1-0 aggregate victory.

31 March 2007

Liverpool take an early lead with a well-crafted goal that starts with Jermaine Pennant's back-heel releasing Álvaro Arbeloa on the right flank, and his low cross is slid home from close range by Peter Crouch to put the Reds 1-0 up.

11 April 2009

Title-chasing Liverpool, with the added desire to win for the Anfield faithful ahead of the 20th anniversary of the 96 fans who died at Hillsborough, take an early lead against Blackburn in spectacular style, as Fernando Torres controls a long pass out of defence on his chest before swivelling and volleying a superb shot past Rovers keeper Paul Robinson to put the Reds 1-0 up.

4 December 2013

Norwich City's Leroy Fer's misplaced pass doesn't look like too much of an issue when Luis Suarez collects the ball midway inside the Canaries half – but the Uruguayan allows it to bounce once in his path before unleashing a shot from almost 40 yards out that flies past keeper John Ruddy and into the top corner. A stunning goal and his first of four goals that evening.

20 April 2014

Raheem Sterling takes just four minutes to put Liverpool ahead away to Norwich City. The young winger cuts inside past a couple of challenges before hitting a ferocious rising shot into the top left-hand corner from 20 yards out to put Brendan Rodgers's title-chasing side 1-0 up.

5

16 April 2001

In the Merseyside derby at Goodison Park Emile Heskey races clear after chasing a through pass and the Reds striker outmuscles Steve Watson, keeps his cool, and then hits a low drive past Paul Gerrard from the edge of the box to give his side an early lead.

23 November 2013

The Reds get off to a flying start in what will be a thrilling Merseyside derby at Goodison Park. As a corner comes in from the left, Luis Suarez flicks the ball on, and Philippe Coutinho gets enough connection to put Liverpool ahead – not his most spectacular effort but they all count!

9 April 2019

Liverpool get off to the perfect start in the first leg of the Champions League quarter-final against Porto. A fine move finishes when Roberto Firmino finds Naby Keita on the edge of the box, and Keita fires a shot that takes a wicked deflection on its way into the back of the net.

6

12 April 1978

Liverpool make the perfect start to the European Cup semi-final second leg against Borussia Mönchengladbach. Trailing 2-1 from the first leg in Germany, the Reds look to level the aggregate as soon as possible, and just six minutes in, Ray Kennedy turns the Anfield volume up to max as Kenny Dalglish spots his run towards goal and sends a cross to the far post, where Kennedy heads home to make it 1-0.

15 April 1989

The referee halts the FA Cup semi-final between Liverpool and Nottingham Forest at Hillsborough. In what will develop into the darkest day in the club's history, 96 Liverpool fans lose their lives at the Leppings Lane end of the ground. The match is abandoned as the horrific events unfold.

17 March 2004

With the Reds looking to get an early advantage against struggling Portsmouth, Michael Owen collects the ball on the left flank. He looks up and spots Didi Hamann's run towards the box and plays a smart, high ball towards the German, and Hamann arrives with perfect timing to hit an unstoppable volley past the Pompey keeper from 20 yards – a stunning goal.

13 April 2014

With Liverpool looking to get a decisive advantage over Manchester City in the Premier League title race, Luis Suarez plays a low pass towards Raheem Sterling and the Reds winger stops the ball, shimmies left, then right, and having sent Vincent Kompany and Joe Hart the wrong way, plants the ball into the empty net to make it 1-0.

30 October 2019

Shkodran Mustafi inadvertently gives Liverpool the lead at the start of what will be an unforgettable Carabao Cup tie at Anfield. Alex Oxlade-Chamberlain flies down the right flank before crossing in low towards Rhian Brewster, but Mustafi's desperate attempt to clear results in an own goal to put the Reds 1-0 up.

10 November 2019

Liverpool break with purpose as Manchester City appeal a handball decision against Trent Alexander-Arnold, and as the ball is played infield to Fabinho, the Brazilian tees himself up before unleashing a 20-yard piledriver that gives Claudio Bravo no chance, in a crucial top-of-the-table clash at Anfield.

4 December 2019

Divock Origi puts Liverpool ahead in the Merseyside derby. Sadio Mané plays a clever pass in behind the Everton defence, and the Belgian's first touch takes him past the goalkeeper and a defender in one move, and leaves him with the simple task of rolling the ball into the empty net to put the Reds 1-0 up.

7

18 April 1964

Knowing victory will bring a sixth top-flight title back to Anfield, the scene is set for the home clash with Arsenal and the gates locked an hour before kick-off. The teams had met earlier in the season in a bad-tempered affair at Highbury and this proves an equally bruising affair. The first goal is always going to be crucial and it is a fine team effort that puts Liverpool ahead, as Roger Hunt avoids a nasty challenge before passing to Alf Arrowsmith, who in turn edges the ball across to Ian St John, who slides it past the keeper to lift the roof off the Kop and put the Reds 1-0 up.

21 November 1998

A breathless start by the Reds. Michael Owen finds Jamie Redknapp on the right of the Aston Villa box, and in turn, he dinks a cross to Robbie Fowler who sends a bullet header into the bottom left-hand corner to put Liverpool 2-0 up at Villa Park.

23 March 1991

Jan Mølby puts Liverpool ahead in what will be a memorable afternoon away to Derby County. Despite the events that follow, future Liverpool defender Mark Wright is penalised for pulling Ian Rush back in the box and the referee awards a penalty. Mølby steps up to calmly slot the ball past Peter Shilton – though there will be plenty more to come. It is also the Reds' 6,000th goal in all competitions.

21 November 2015

The first real sign that Jürgen Klopp is a very special Normal One, as the Reds begin a dismantling mission on Manchester City at the Etihad Stadium. Philippe Coutinho wins possession on the left flank before playing a pass to Roberto Firmino in the City box – the Brazilian immediately fires a low ball into the six-yard box where Eliaquim Mangala puts the ball past Joe Hart for an own goal to put Liverpool in front.

5 May 2016

Liverpool get an early bonus against Villarreal in the semi-final second leg of the Europa League at Anfield. Trailing 1-0 from the first leg in Spain, the Reds attack the Kop and are ahead from almost the first attack, as Nathaniel Clyne's low cross skims across the six-yard box to the left of the box where Roberto Firmino immediately puts the ball in the danger zone and Bruno Soriano can't help but deflect the cross past his own keeper to level the aggregate score at 1-1.

7 May 2019

The start Liverpool need in the Champions League semi-final second leg with Barcelona. Trailing 3-0 from the first leg, the Reds need the perfect start – and it comes when Jordan Henderson powers his way into the Barça box before hitting a low shot that Marc-André ter Stegen saves, but he only pushes the ball into the path of Divock Origi to make it 1-0.

8

18 February 1896

Malcolm McVean opens the scoring for Liverpool against Rotherham United at Anfield in what will be a memorable day for the Reds. McVean goes on to complete a hat-trick in nine minutes against the Millers, as Liverpool eventually win 10-1.

2 September 1978

Kenny Dalglish puts Liverpool on the way to a big win over Tottenham at Anfield. The Scotland striker expertly holds off his marker in the box before spinning and firing a low shot home from close range to put the Reds 1-0 up.

12 September 1989

Steve Nicol opens the scoring against Crystal Palace. John Barnes sees his attempt blocked before the ball falls to Ronnie Whelan on the edge of the box – the Republic of Ireland midfielder cleverly flicks the ball to his right and Nicol fires a right-foot shot home from 15 yards to put the Reds on the way to a 9-0 win.

3 March 1996

A stunning Robbie Fowler goal to cap a stunning Liverpool start against Aston Villa at Anfield. The Reds are already 2-0 up when Fowler collects a pass midway inside the Villa half, loses marker Steve Staunton with a Cruyff turn, then hits a left-foot rising piledriver that flies past Villa keeper Mark Bosnich to put the Reds 3-0 up with only eight minutes played.

22 March 2009

Liverpool's late surge for the title gets a huge boost when Dirk Kuyt gives the Reds an early lead at Anfield. Steven Gerrard whips in a free kick from 25 yards and after an Aston Villa head deflects it on to the crossbar, the ball drops kindly for Kuyt, who makes no mistake from close range.

9

31 August 2006

Liverpool take an early lead in the 2006 FA Community Shield against Chelsea at the Millennium Stadium in Cardiff. John Arne Riise races fully 60 yards before hitting a dipping shot over Carlo Cudicini to put the Reds in control.

29 October 2011

Charlie Adam tucks away his first Liverpool goal away to West Brom. The Reds go on to win the game 2-0 at The Hawthorns and move to fifth in the Premier League, ten points behind leaders Manchester City. It is one of only two goals the Scottish midfielder will score for the Reds in 37 appearances.

13 January 2016

Liverpool take an early lead against Arsenal at Anfield. James Milner finds Emre Can on the edge of the box, and the German unleashes a powerful low drive that Petr Cech can only push into the path of Roberto Firmino, who makes no mistake from close range.

2 May 2018

Liverpool get just the start they need to bat off any AS Roma hopes of a shock victory. Leading 5-2 from the first leg at Anfield, Roberto Firmino intercepts a loose ball, drives forward, before sliding a pass to his left, where Sadio Mané makes no mistake from ten yards out.

2 October 2019

A quite wonderful goal from Sadio Mané, who creates a goal out of nothing against Red Bull Salzburg. The Senegalese striker picks up the ball on the left before drifting in towards the edge of the box, playing a one-two with Roberto Firmino, and slotting the ball home with an angled shot to make it 1-0. A goal from a player at the very peak of his powers.

10

12 April 1909

Liverpool bolster their chances of escaping relegation with a fine 3-0 win over third-placed Sunderland at Anfield. Ronald Orr tucks home a penalty on ten minutes after Albert Milton's handball to give the Reds the lead, and the goal means a notable landmark is reached as it is the club's 1,000th in all competitions.

25 November 1964

Ian St John becomes the first Liverpool player to score in the new all-red home kit. Bill Shankly's thinking that playing in just one colour, instead of having white shorts and white socks, would make his team look stronger just happens to be at the very start of the club's most successful period ever. St John's goal comes against Anderlecht at Anfield in the European Cup first round first leg, and the Reds – as they emphatically are now – go on to win 3-0.

5 April 2005

Liverpool make the perfect start in the Champions League quarter-final first leg against Juventus at Anfield. Steven Gerrard's corner is flicked on at the near post and Sami Hyypiä arrives at the far post to send a left-foot volley past Gianluigi Buffon to give the Reds a vital early advantage against the Italians.

26 October 2008

Xabi Alonso scores what proves to be the only goal of the game in a top-of-the-table Premier League clash at Stamford Bridge. The Spaniard's shot takes a wicked deflection of Bosingwa, wrong-footing Petr Cech, and ends up in the back of the net. It's Alonso's first goal for a year, and more importantly, the 1-0 win puts the Reds top of the table and ends Chelsea's incredible 86-game unbeaten home run stretching back four years in the process.

14 January 2018

Unbeaten Manchester City see their long unbeaten run end in a classic encounter at Anfield. The Blues arrive on Merseyside 18 points ahead of the Reds with 22 games played, but Jürgen Klopp's side are keen to prove a point. Picking up the ball midway into the City half, Alex Oxlade-Chamberlain drives past one challenge before arrowing a 25-yard shot past Ederson to give Liverpool an early lead.

11

22 August 1964

Roger Hunt puts Liverpool ahead against Arsenal at Anfield. The striker's goal is seen by thousands more eyes than normal, with the match being shown on the BBC's new football show *Match of the Day*, and will end in a thrilling 3-2 win for the Reds.

21 August 1971

Liverpool take the lead against Newcastle United at St James' Park with a long-range goal from Emlyn Hughes. Steve Heighway's cross is headed clear by a Magpies defender and the ball comes out to Hughes, who cushions it on his chest before firing a left-foot volley over the keeper and into the roof of the net from 20 yards.

6 November 1982

Alan Hansen anticipates an Everton pass and intercepts, before moving forward into the Everton half with purpose, splitting the Toffees defence with a superb pass to Ian Rush, who fires a left-foot shot past Neville Southall to put Liverpool ahead.

25 April 1984

Ian Rush scores a vital early away goal as Liverpool open up a 2-0 aggregate lead in the second leg of the 1984 European Cup semi-final against Dinamo Bucharest. As the ball is played into the Bucharest box, Rush controls it, takes it past a defender, and as the keeper runs towards him, the Welsh striker dinks the ball over him and into the back of the net to give the Reds a vital away goal.

16 September 1990

A lovely sweeping move between Steve McMahon and John Barnes sees the latter cross low into the box, and McMahon's contribution almost causes an own goal, but Manchester United goalkeeper Les Sealey pushes the ball clear before Peter Beardsley reacts quickly to poke it into the net and put Liverpool ahead in the First Division clash at Anfield.

13 April 1991

Liverpool take an early lead at Elland Road as Ian Rush finds John Barnes on the edge of the Leeds United box, and the England winger cleverly dinks the ball over a static Leeds defence for Ray Houghton to have the simplest of chances to side-foot home in this War of the Roses First Division clash.

15 September 2001

Trailing 1-0 after just five minutes, the Reds roar back quickly against Everton at Goodison Park. A cross into the Toffees box is half cleared, but only as far as Steven Gerrard, who collects the loose ball, shimmies past a defender, before arrowing an unstoppable rising shot past Tim Howard to make it 1-1.

28 December 2005

As Liverpool attack, a game of head tennis ensues between the teams that ends with Steven Gerrard nodding the ball into Peter Crouch's path, and the Reds striker races clear before skipping around Nigel Martyn and tucking a low shot into the empty net to give Liverpool the lead in the Merseyside derby at Goodison Park.

9 December 2012

After picking the ball up on the right deep in the West Ham half, Glen Johnson accelerates past one challenge and heads for the Hammers box. With several defenders blocking his path, Johnson cuts across the ball as he hits a powerful rising shot that arrows into the top left-hand corner to put the Reds on their way at Upton Park.

1 March 2015

Title-chasing Manchester City arrive at Anfield looking for a rare away win against Liverpool, but just 11 minutes in, the visitors realise it perhaps isn't going to be their day, as Jordan Henderson collects a pass on the edge of the City box before shifting right slightly and unleashing a superb curling effort into the top right-hand corner of Joe Hart's net. They may be collectors' items, but a Henderson goal is usually worth the wait.

12

29 December 1928

Gordon Hodgson puts Liverpool ahead against Bury. Though the game is nothing particularly special in terms of club history, Hodgson's goal is the Reds' 2,000th in all competitions, and Hodgson adds another after the break in the 2-2 draw at Gigg Lane.

14 August 1971

Kevin Keegan scores on his Liverpool debut to get his career with the Reds off to a flying start. John Toshack gets the first of many assists for the diminutive forward – who arrived for just £35,000 from Scunthorpe United – as he touches on a cross that Keegan sweeps home from close range.

1 January 2001

What a way to start the new year. Steven Gerrard collects the ball midway inside the Southampton half before looking up for possible options ahead of him. He then decides 'why not?', tees himself up, before unleashing a ferocious shot into the top right-hand corner of the Saints net from fully 35 yards out. Truly world class from Stevie G.

29 November 2009

The Reds are looking for a third successive win at Goodison Park. The ball is played to Javier Mascherano

30 yards out, and the Argentine fires a shot that deflects of Joseph Yobo to wrong-foot Tim Howard completely and give Liverpool a 1-0 lead.

13

30 March 1976

John Toshack silences the Camp Nou as he drills a low shot past Pedro Mora and into the bottom corner of the net from 15 yards to put Liverpool 1-0 up in the UEFA Cup semi-final first leg.

16 April 1983

Kenny Dalglish levels the score for Liverpool away to Southampton. The Reds eventually lose 3-2 at The Dell. Manchester United could still have won the league at this point as they had three matches in hand over Liverpool and still eight points to play in the season. Liverpool were champions two matches later after losing at Spurs when United only drew against Norwich.

30 May 1984

The 1984 European Cup Final in Rome and the Reds are taking on AS Roma in their own stadium. Despite the disadvantage and partisan home crowd, Liverpool take the lead on 13 minutes. Graeme Souness and Sammy Lee exchange passes before finding Craig Johnston on the right. He plays a high cross into the Roma penalty area, goalkeeper Franco Tancredi and Ronnie Whelan compete for the ball, Tancredi gets there first, spills the ball, and as Roma desperately try to clear the danger, Michele Nappi's attempted clearance bounces off Tancredi's back and falls to Phil Neal, who scores to give Liverpool a 1-0 lead.

5 October 1993

An unforgettable night for Robbie Fowler as the Reds take on Fulham in the League Cup at Anfield. Rob Jones tries his luck from 35 yards out and his low effort is pushed out as far as Fowler, who makes no mistake from close range.

11 April 2011

Liverpool put a massive dent in Manchester City's hopes of Champions League qualification with an inspired performance at Anfield. The opening goal comes from Andy Carroll – his first for the Reds – with the former Newcastle United striker fizzing a low half-volley from 20 yards that gives Joe Hart no chance.

11 January 2012

Liverpool take a vital lead in the League Cup semi-final first leg at the Etihad Stadium. The referee judges that Stefan Savic has fouled Daniel Agger, and Steven Gerrard tucks the penalty home for what will prove the only goal of the game.

4 April 2018

Liverpool draw first blood in the all-English Champions League quarter-final first leg at Anfield. Robert Firmino sees his low shot saved by Ederson and the ball falls to Kyle Walker, who gets tangled up, allowing Firmino to stab the ball across the six-yard box, and Mo Salah emphatically finishes to send the Kop wild.

10 November 2019

Mo Salah doubles Liverpool's lead against Manchester City. In a crucial top-of-the-table clash at Anfield, Andy Robertson receives the ball and immediately drives forward, before sending in a cross that Salah heads home past Claudio Bravo to make it 2-0.

14

Boxing Day 2005

Steven Gerrard cheers the festive Anfield crowd with a typically superb goal. Gerrard picks up a knock-down pass outside the box before skipping past one challenge into the area, and as three defenders close in, he unleashes a fearsome shot into the top left-hand corner to put the Reds 1-0 up.

28 October 2012

Luis Suarez plays a big part in Liverpool taking the lead at Goodison Park. José Enrique drives into the Everton box before firing a cross into the six-yard box, where Raheem Sterling is inches away from connecting – but Suarez collects the loose ball and hits a low shot that hits Leighton Baines and ends up in the back of the net for the opening goal of the game.

29 December 2018

Arsenal's bright start has seen them go ahead on 11 minutes at Anfield, but within five minutes, Roberto Firmino puts the Reds in front. His first comes when he starts an attack with purpose, finding Mo Salah whose cross should be cut out – but the Arsenal defending is awful, and the ball rolls back into Firmino's path after a series of deflections.

15

3 September 1892

Liverpool's first official recorded goal comes on 15 minutes as Jock Smith scores against Higher Walton in a Lancashire League clash at Anfield. The Reds go on to win 8-0, but it is Smith's name that goes into the history books, with Liverpool FC officially up and running.

23 November 1946

Chasing a unique and remarkable feat, Jack Balmer puts Liverpool ahead against Arsenal at Anfield. Balmer, who has scored a hat-trick in his previous two games against Portsmouth and Derby County, tucks home a penalty to give the First Division leaders the perfect start.

15 August 1964

Another historic first after 15 minutes, when Phil Chisnall becomes the first recorded substitute for Liverpool as he replaces Alf Arrowsmith in the FA Charity Shield clash with West Ham United at Anfield. Arrowsmith injures his knee but has returned to try to play on, when his knee gives way and he collapses in agony. It is Chisnall's debut.

14 August 1971

Kevin Keegan's Liverpool debut gets even better as the Reds new boy – who has scored against Nottingham Forest three minutes earlier – wins a penalty after being tripped in the box by Liam O'Kane, and Tommy Smith makes no mistake from the spot.

19 May 1976

Kevin Keegan drills home a low free kick to equalise against Club Bruges in the second leg of the UEFA Cup Final. The goal proves to be enough to secure the trophy for the second time, with the Reds holding on for a 1-1 draw to win 4-3 on aggregate.

3 May 1977

Kevin Keegan rises to score his 100th Liverpool goal in all competitions and his final one for the Reds. The industrious forward rises to meet David Johnson's perfect cross to head powerfully past Alex Stepney in the Manchester United goal to send Anfield wild. It proves to be the only goal of the game and leaves Bob Paisley's side needing just four points from the remaining four games to be crowned First Division champions (which, of course, they achieve comfortably). For Keegan, however, it's the end of an era for a player who joined as an unknown in 1971 but leaves a superstar some 323 games and six years later.

21 September 1996

Premier League leaders Liverpool take on third-placed Chelsea with both teams defending unbeaten starts to the campaign. The Reds get the start they need when Stig Inge Bjørnebye advances into the Chelsea half before sending a peach of a left-foot cross into the box, where Robbie Fowler meets it full on to send a bullet header past Kevin Hitchcock to make it 1-0.

31 March 2001

In a powder-keg atmosphere at Anfield, it's the Merseyside Reds who draw first blood. The ball is nodded to Robbie Fowler who cushions a pass to Steven Gerrard, and the young midfielder only has one thing in his mind as he nudges the ball forward before hitting a fearsome shot from 30 yards out into the top left-hand corner of the United net to send the home fans wild.

12 August 2001

Liverpool double their lead on the quarter hour in the FA Charity Shield clash with Manchester United. Emile Heskey attempts to jump for a long pass forward and Michael Owen reacts first to the loose ball, turning Gary Neville inside out before driving home a low shot from 15 yards to make it 2-0.

16

13 April 1991

Jan Mølby strokes home a penalty against Leeds United to put the Reds 2-0 up in the First Division clash at Elland Road, after great work from Ian Rush and John Barnes had earned the spot kick.

20 January 1998

As a deep cross comes into the Newcastle United box, Michael Owen brings down the ball superbly with his chest before sending an angled shot into the top corner for what proves to be the only goal of a tight game at Anfield.

31 March 2001

Robbie Fowler lays off a short pass midway inside the Manchester United half, and Steven Gerrard takes a touch to line up his sights before unleashing a ferocious drive into the top left-hand corner from 30 yards out, giving Fabian Barthez no chance and putting the Reds 1-0 up against United.

16 May 2001

Liverpool go 2-0 up in the UEFA Cup Final against Alavés. Michael Owen receives the ball midway inside the Spaniards' half, moves forward and then threads a ball into the path of Steven Gerrard, who hits a powerful low shot past the keeper from just inside the box.

15 March 2006

Robbie Fowler scores his first goal since rejoining Liverpool. The Reds legend, nicknamed 'God' by the supporters, heads home at the far post, after Harry Kewell's corner is flicked on by Luis Garcia, to make it 1-0 against Fulham at a delighted Anfield.

10 March 2009

In the days before VAR, Fernando Torres possibly gets away with not one but two fouls in the build-up to a crucial opening goal against Real Madrid at Anfield. Leading 1-0 from the first leg of the round of 16 clash, Torres chases a long ball and collides with one defender, before appearing to pull back another as he continues into the box – that leaves Dirk Kuyt free to square the loose ball across the six-yard box for Torres to score from close range. Would it have stood today? Probably not, but it gives the Reds the perfect platform for a memorable night under the Anfield lights ...

29 December 2018

Having just got the title-chasing Reds back on level terms, Roberto Firmino scores his second goal in three minutes with a sublime individual effort. The Brazilian slaloms past two challenges before sending another defender on to his backside, before lashing a shot past the keeper to send Anfield wild and put Liverpool 2-1 in front against Arsenal at Anfield.

31 March 2019

Roberto Firmino puts Liverpool 1-0 up against Spurs at Anfield. Andy Robertson whips a curling cross in towards the six-yard box, and Firmino arrives on cue to send his header low and hard past Hugo Lloris to give the Reds the lead.

17

17 November 1973

Kevin Keegan gets the first of his three goals against Ipswich Town to put Liverpool 1-0 up. It's no surprise that the assist comes from John Toshack, who fires a cross towards the far post, and Keegan bravely dives in to head home from three yards out.

1 October 1974

Already leading 11-0 from the first leg in the European Cup Winners' Cup first round, Ray Kennedy puts Liverpool in front against Strømsgodset at the Ullevaal Stadion in Norway – but the hosts, playing for pride only, are much better than their Anfield showing and the Reds settle for a single-goal victory and a clean sheet.

3 February 2002

Liverpool's Premier League title hopes get a boost with a handsome win at Elland Road against Leeds United. Danny Murphy fires a curling free kick into the Leeds box from the left flank and it is Rio Ferdinand who glances the ball past his own keeper to give the Reds a 1-0 lead.

16 September 2016

Liverpool edge ahead at Stamford Bridge against Chelsea as Dejan Lovren volleys the Reds in front from close range. Philippe Coutinho is the creator as he sends a cross in from the left to where three Liverpool players are queuing up, but it's Lovren who gets there first with a controlled shot from six yards out.

12 May 2019

For at least ten minutes, Liverpool fans can believe the title dream might actually be becoming a reality. Needing to better Manchester City's result on the final day of the greatest title race of all time, Sadio Mané drills home Trent Alexander-Arnold's low cross from the right to put the Reds ahead of City in the live table.

4 December 2019

Xherdan Shaqiri doubles Liverpool's lead against Everton following a superb piece of play by Sadio Mané. Mané cuts in from the left before playing a threaded reverse pass into the path of Shaqiri, who slides in to direct the ball past Jordan Pickford and put the Reds 2-0 up at Anfield.

18

13 April 1988

Liverpool take the lead against Nottingham Forest with a superb goal by Ray Houghton. The Republic of Ireland midfielder drives into space in the Forest half before playing a one-two with John Barnes, skipping past another challenge inside the box, and then slotting a low shot home to make it 1-0 at Anfield.

28 December 2005

After assisting for the opening goal, Steven Gerrard grabs the second for himself to put the Reds 2-0 up at Goodison Park. Collecting a headed clearance 25 yards out, Gerrard fires a low shot that Nigel Martyn doesn't see until the ball nestles in the back of the net.

20 January 2007

Leading 1-0 against second-placed Chelsea thanks to a fourth-minute goal from Dirk Kuyt, a cross into the Chelsea box is cleared to the corner of the area, where Jermaine Pennant tees himself up before unleashing a dipping, angled shot into the top left-hand corner of Petr Cech's goal to double the Reds' lead.

15 December 2013

Luis Suarez shows tenacity and superb close control as he puts Liverpool on the way to a big win against Tottenham Hotspur at White Hart Lane. The Uruguayan's pass to Jordan Henderson is cut out in the Spurs box, but Henderson manages to poke the ball back to Suarez, who reacts fastest to dribble past one challenge before tucking a low shot home to give the Reds a 1-0 lead.

23 January 2016

Bobby Firmino scores the first goal of what will be an extraordinary game at Carrow Road. The Brazilian gets in behind the Norwich City defence before sending a low angled shot in off the far post to put the Reds 1-0 up.

30 November 2019

Virgil van Dijk puts Liverpool ahead against Brighton and Hove Albion at Anfield. Trent Alexander-Arnold's superb cross from the right is met with a towering header from van Dijk to put the Reds ahead.

19

21 April 1962

Liverpool look to confirm what has seemed likely for some time, as Bill Shankly's side look for victory over Southampton that will confirm the Second Division title. Injury to Ian St John means that Kevin Lewis starts – and the 21-year-old takes his chance, converting a shot in off the underside of the crossbar, after an almighty scramble in the six-yard box, to put the Reds on their way.

10 August 1974

Phil Boersma scrambles the ball into the net from close range after Kevin Keegan's shot has been fumbled by Leeds United keeper David Harvey to put the Reds ahead in a feisty FA Charity Shield clash at Wembley Stadium.

15 March 2008

Reading are proving to be difficult opponents in 2007/08, having already beaten Liverpool 3-1 at home earlier in the campaign. When the Royals go ahead on five minutes at Anfield, it seems as though the Reds might be on the way to an unwanted Premier League double, but Javier Mascherano has other ideas, and after collecting the ball halfway inside the Reading half, the Argentine drifts inside one challenge before lashing a shot past the keeper from 20 yards to make it 1-1.

14 April 2009

Fabio Aurelio's quick thinking gives Liverpool a vital lead at Stamford Bridge. Trailing 3-1 from the Champions League quarter-final first leg at Anfield, Aurelio shapes up to send a 35-yard free kick in from the right flank, but instead he spots Petr Cech on the left of his goal line and whips a low shot in with his left foot that curls into the bottom right-hand corner, putting the Reds 1-0 up on the night.

6 November 2007

Peter Crouch grabs the opening goal against Besiktas at Anfield. Crouch will also score the final goal in the record 8-0 Champions League victory against the Turks. The margin is also a competition record at that stage, too.

23 November 2013

Despite going ahead after just five minutes, Everton level on eight minutes in a thrilling Merseyside derby at Goodison Park. But when the Reds are awarded a free kick 25 yards out, it is perfect territory for Philippe Coutinho or Luis Suarez, and it is Suarez who strikes low around the wall and into the net to make it 2-1.

8 May 2012

A pumped-up Liverpool take on Chelsea just three days after the Blues have triumphed in the FA Cup Final. Keen to get instant payback, Luis Suarez dances past one challenge on the right and moves into the box at speed, until he hits the ball across from close range and Michael

Essien can only deflect it into his own net to put the Reds 1-0 up.

13 January 2016

Liverpool retake the lead against Arsenal and Roberto Firmino scores his second of the game. Arsenal have made it 1-1 a few minutes before and the Reds look to try to re-establish a grip on the game. James Milner finds himself in space on the edge of the box before playing it to his right, where Firmino curls an absolute beauty into the top right-hand corner to make it 2-1.

20

28 April 1894

Patrick Gordon puts Liverpool 1-0 up against Newton Heath (later to become Manchester United) in a Test Match at Ewood Park. Liverpool had won the Second Division, while Newton Heath had finished bottom of the First Division. The result is a match that would decide promotion, relegation – or neither. Gordon's goal, however, puts Liverpool on their way to a 2-0 win and promotion to the top division and relegates Newton Heath as a result. A rivalry is well and truly born!

29 April 1901

Johnny Walker's solitary goal is enough to beat West Bromwich Albion 1-0 at The Hawthorns and seal a first-ever league title for Liverpool. Though the Baggies are bottom and facing relegation, the Reds have to work hard for the victory, which leaves them two points clear of Sunderland at the top and champions at last!

1 September 1906

A momentous day as Liverpool play in front of the new Spion Kop for the first time. Playing against Stoke City in searing heat, Joe Hewitt scores the only goal of the game as the Reds start the 1906/07 season with a narrow 1-0 win.

16 April 1977

Phil Neal hits a 25-yard shot into the bottom left-hand corner to put the Reds ahead against Arsenal. Playing a side who haven't lost at Anfield since 1972, the breakthrough comes when Neal has a punt from distance and the ball somehow manages to beat Jimmy Rimmer with a deflection on its way.

2 September 1978

Kenny Dalglish scores his second of the game against Tottenham after an almighty scramble in the box. Several crosses and shots are scrambled clear before the ball falls to Jimmy Case on the edge of the box – Case's low drive is going wide before Dalglish diverts it into the net from six yards to put the Reds 2-0 up.

5 October 1997

Patrik Berger scores the first of a hat-trick against Chelsea at Anfield with a clever finish. Paul Ince's long ball sees Chelsea defender Graeme Le Saux fooled by the backspin of the ball, and Berger judges it to perfection before calmly lobbing the keeper from 15 yards to put the Reds 1-0 up.

28 October 2012

After assisting for the first goal, Luis Suarez scores the second himself to put Liverpool 2-0 up at Goodison Park. After Raheem Sterling is fouled 30 yards from goal, Steven Gerrard whips in a free kick that Suarez heads past Tim Howard with the slightest of touches, to put the Reds firmly in command in the Merseyside derby.

23 February 2014

Already leading 1-0 from Daniel Sturridge's early goal, the Reds double their advantage with a sublime goal from Jordan Henderson. Luis Suarez plays Sturridge in down the right flank and his short pass finds Henderson on the edge of the Swansea box, where he strikes an inch-perfect shot into the top left-hand corner from 20 yards out.

10 March 2016

Liverpool get a vital early lead against Manchester United in the Europa League round of 16 first leg at Anfield. Nathaniel Clyne races on to a pass in the box, but Memphis Depay clips his heels and the referee awards a penalty that Daniel Sturridge confidently rolls home to put the Reds deservedly 1-0 up on the night.

17 December 2017

Philippe Coutinho drifts into the Bournemouth penalty area from the left, goes by one challenge and then, with several defenders closing in, he hits a low drive into the bottom corner to put the Reds in front at the Vitality Stadium.

27 February 2019

Sadio Mané has already put Liverpool ahead against Watford on nine minutes when he doubles the advantage with the most impudent of finishes. Trent Alexander-Arnold's cross picks out an unmarked Mané, but the Senegalese striker's first touch takes him away from goal, so with his back to the goalkeeper, he back-heels a shot that completely takes Ben Foster by surprise, with what is a quite brilliant piece of improvisation.

21

10 May 1973

Chris Lawler's deep cross into the Borussia Mönchengladbach box finds the head of John Toshack, and the Welshman nods the ball across the box towards Kevin Keegan, who powers a header into the far corner of the net, wrong-footing Wolfgang Kleff to give the Reds the lead in the UEFA Cup Final first leg at Anfield.

6 December 1977

In the second leg of the European Super Cup against Kevin Keegan's Hamburg, Phil Thompson puts the Reds ahead. After seeing his header blocked from a corner, Thompson is first to react with a snapshot from close range that makes it 1-0 at Anfield, and 2-1 on aggregate.

28 March 1984

In a tense League Cup Final replay at Manchester City's Maine Road, Graeme Souness scores what proves to be the only goal of the game against Everton. Phil Neal slides a pass into the feet of Souness, who flips the ball up slightly before turning quickly and firing a powerful left-foot shot past Neville Southall from 30 yards out.

5 October 1993

Robbie Fowler scores his second of the night against Fulham in the League Cup. The Reds are awarded an indirect free kick on the edge of the Fulham six-yard box, and a well-worked free-kick routine sees Neil Ruddock shape up to blast the ball, but instead he passes it sideways where Fowler squeezes the ball inside the far post from close range.

1 November 1999

The ball is played to Titi Camara midway inside the Bradford City half. The Reds striker controls the pass, turns and nutmegs his marker, before striding a few paces forward and drilling a low left-foot shot past the keeper from 18 yards.

29 February 2004

Harry Kewell celebrates a leap year goal with a sublime effort at Elland Road against his former club Leeds United. The Australian tries his luck from the right of the Leeds box, and his curling left-foot shot beats the keeper and goes into the top left of the Leeds United goal to make it 1-0 to the Reds.

28 January 2014

Liverpool draw first blood in the Merseyside derby. Luis Suarez whips in a corner from the left, and who else but captain fantastic Steven Gerrard rises higher than anyone else to nod the ball into the top-left corner to put the Reds ahead at Anfield.

4 April 2018

Liverpool double their lead in the all-English Champions League quarter-final first leg at Anfield. Roberto Firmino appeals for a foul as City scramble the ball clear, but it only falls for Alex Oxlade-Chamberlain, who hits a thunderous rising shot past Ederson from 18 yards out to put the Reds firmly in control.

22

17 April 1922

Harry Chambers puts Liverpool ahead against defending First Division champions Burnley at Anfield. If results go the Reds' way, they could be crowned champions with a victory ... fast forward to minute 78 to discover what happens ...

17 November 1973

Kevin Keegan scores his second of the game against Ipswich Town. Steve Heighway glides towards goal on the left, beats a defender and then sends a cross towards the near post, where Keegan arrives first to head home from close range and put the Reds 2-0 up.

16 September 1995

Robbie Fowler doubles Liverpool's lead over Blackburn Rovers at Anfield. Already 1-0 up from Jamie Redknapp's goal, Fowler nips in between two Rovers defenders to meet Rob Jones's cross with a diving header to make it 2-0. It is yet another blow for the defending Premier League champions, who have taken just four out of a possible 18 points from their first six games.

4 November 2017

Mo Salah puts Liverpool ahead at the London Stadium, but it is made by Sadio Mané. Mané races out of his own half towards the Hammers goal, and it is a two-on-one situation with Salah racing alongside him. Mané waits for the right moment before sliding the ball to his right, and Salah coolly controls it before placing a low shot past the keeper to make it 1-0 to the Reds.

23

10 February 1981

Kenny Dalglish gives Liverpool the lead in front of the Kop with a clinical finish and puts the Reds on course for the League Cup Final. Liverpool had won the first leg away to Manchester City and Dalglish's goal makes it 2-0 on aggregate. Though City will later level and hit the woodwork twice, Bob Paisley's men hold on to progress to Wembley.

3 May 1986

Liverpool are crowned First Division champions at Stamford Bridge. Needing a win to guarantee a 16th title, the Reds make the breakthrough when Ronnie Whelan nods the ball towards the Chelsea box, Ian Rush helps it into the path of player-manager Kenny Dalglish, and he expertly controls the ball with his chest before placing a low volley to the right of the keeper for what proves to be the only goal of the game.

23 March 1991

Liverpool regain the lead away to Derby County. With both teams having converted a penalty, the Reds attack with Ian Rush and John Barnes combining to see Rush hit a low shot that is pushed out by Peter Shilton – but only as far as Barnes, who tucks the loose ball home from a tight angle to make it 2-1.

24 August 2001

John Arne Riise puts Liverpool ahead in the European Super Cup at the Stade Louis II in Monaco. Michael Owen is sent scampering down the right flank, and his cross into the box is met at the far post with a low finish from Riise to give the Reds the lead against Bayern Munich.

21 November 2015

Liverpool make it 2-0 against title-chasing Manchester City at the Etihad with a goal from a player who loves scoring against the Blues. Great work by Roberto Firmino sees the Brazilian play a clever pass behind the City defence for Philippe Coutinho to slot home from eight yards.

23 September 2017

Having lost against Leicester City just four days earlier in the League Cup, the Reds are back at the King Power Stadium looking for payback in the Premier League. Liverpool's start blows the Foxes away, and after Mo Salah's early goal, Philippe Coutinho whips a 25-yard free kick up and over the Leicester wall and into the top corner of the net for his customary 'worldy' goal.

20 October 2018

An edgy Liverpool travel to Huddersfield Town looking for three points to maintain their title challenge with Manchester City. Midway through the first half, Trent Alexander-Arnold spots Mo Salah's run and curls a superb pass over the top for the Egyptian to run on to and lob the ball over the home keeper for what proves to be the only goal of a nervy Reds display.

24

3 August 2013

Joe Allen puts Liverpool ahead in Steven Gerrard's testimonial game against Olympiacos at Anfield. The Reds legend is given a rousing day to remember, with 44,362 fans coming to pay homage to one of the club's greatest players. Jordan Henderson will add another after the break in a 2-0 win over the Greek side.

4 November 2017

Liverpool make it two goals in two minutes at the London Stadium. Mo Salah's corner is deflected towards his own goal by Mark Noble and though Joe Hart pushes the ball out, Jöel Matip is on hand to prod home the rebound and make it 2-0 to the Reds against West Ham United.

16 December 2018

Sadio Mané gives Liverpool the lead against Manchester United at Anfield. After fluffing a couple of chances, the Reds make the breakthrough, as Fabinho picks out Mané's run into the box and the Senegalese striker expertly cushions the pass with his chest before firing past David de Gea to make it 1-0.

30 November 2019

Virgil van Dijk scores his second goal in six minutes to put the Reds firmly in control against Brighton. Trent Alexander-Arnold again provides the assist, this time from a left-flank corner and the big Dutch defender again is first to the ball, heading past Mat Ryan to make it 2-0.

25

28 August 1971

Steve Heighway draws Liverpool level against Leicester City. The Foxes had taken the lead 60 seconds earlier through a deflected shot, and Heighway's equaliser is almost a carbon copy as he strikes a low shot from the edge of the box that hits a Leicester defender and wrong-foots goalkeeper Peter Shilton to make it 1-1.

1 April 1981

Kenny Dalglish equalises for Liverpool in the 1981 League Cup Final replay at Villa Park. Terry McDermott dinks a ball over the West Ham defence and Dalglish, never taking his eye off the ball, slides in to send an angled volley past the keeper to make it 1-1.

13 April 1991

The Reds run riot at Elland Road with a third inside the first 25 minutes against Leeds United. After a spell of sustained pressure, Ronnie Whelan finds John Barnes on the left, and his low cross into the six-yard box is powered home by David Speedie to make it 3-0 in the First Division clash.

4 January 1994

It is a nightmare scenario for Liverpool fans as Manchester United race into a 3-0 lead at Anfield with only 23 minutes on the clock. But Nigel Clough starts the comeback as he pounces on Roy Keane's weak clearance to hit a low shot just out of the reach of Peter Schmeichel's fingertips from 25 yards out.

5 April 2005

Luis Garcia scores what will prove to be the decisive goal in the Champions League quarter-final first leg with Juventus. The Spaniard controls the ball 25 yards out before unleashing a superb dipping volley into the top-left corner to make it 2-0 on the night. The Reds go on to win 2-1 and a 0-0 draw in Turin a week later books a semi-final spot.

8 May 2012

Jordan Henderson puts Liverpool 2-0 up against Chelsea as the Reds seek revenge for losing the FA Cup Final against the same opponents just a few days before. Maxi Rodriguez plays a pass into the Chelsea half that looks harmless until John Terry slips, and Henderson runs on to the pass before sliding a low shot past Ross Turnbull from the edge of the box.

2 October 2019

Another wonderful goal puts Liverpool 2-0 up against Red Bull Salzburg. It begins with Andy Robertson on the halfway line playing it to Jordan Henderson midway inside the Austrians' half. He plays a one-two with Mo Salah before the Reds skipper spreads the ball wide to Trent Alexander-Arnold, who sprints down the right flank before crossing in low where Robertson, who started the move, meets the ball sweetly with a left-foot shot to double the lead in the Champions League group stage clash.

26

11 April 1984

A rare Sammy Lee header gives the Reds a vital first leg advantage in the European Cup semi-final first leg at Anfield against Dinamo Bucharest. Kenny Dalglish's free kick from the left is headed down by Lee in what proves to be the only goal of the tie.

28 August 1994

A record-breaking day for 19-year-old Liverpool striker Robbie Fowler. In the warm Anfield sunshine, Fowler proves just what a talent he is against the Gunners in fewer than five breathtaking minutes. In a classic master and apprentice moment, a cross into the box finds Ian Rush, who nods the ball down for Fowler to sweep home from six yards and put the Reds 1-0 up.

2 May 2018

Despite having been pegged back by a bizarre James Milner own goal, Liverpool regain the lead in the Stadio Olimpico, as Georginio Wijnaldum nods a wayward AS Roma clearance past Alisson to make it 2-1 and 7-3 on aggregate in a thrilling Champions League semi-final second leg encounter.

13 March 2019

Having been held 0-0 at Anfield in the Champions League round of 16 first leg against Bayern Munich, Sadio Mané scores a crucial away goal at the Allianz Arena to put the Reds 1-0 up. Chasing a superb ball out of defence from Virgil van Dijk, the Liverpool forward controls the ball on the edge of the Bayern box as Manuel Neuer races off his line, but Mané turns the keeper before chipping the ball over a defender and into the far corner of the net. A brilliant piece of skill by the Senegal striker.

9 April 2019

The Reds take a 2-0 lead over Porto at Anfield, as Trent Alexander-Arnold's low cross is tapped home by Roberto Firmino to give Jürgen Klopp's side the upper hand in the Champions League quarter-final first leg.

17 April 2019

Liverpool score in the 26th minute against Porto for the second successive game to all but ensure a place in the Champions League semi-final. The Portuguese side allow Roberto Firmino too much time and space and his low ball finds Sadio Mané, who slides home the first of the night in the Stadium of Light – despite looking suspiciously offside.

27

15 November 1969

Chris Lawler gets the honour of scoring the first goal in colour on *Match of the Day*. The Reds right-back collects the ball from a corner and after controlling it, shoots past the West Ham United keeper to put Liverpool 1-0 up at Anfield.

4 March 2000

Liverpool go ahead at Old Trafford with a breathtaking goal. Awarded a free kick 35 yards out, Patrik Berger decides to have a go and cracks a superb shot that Raimond van der Gouw can't do anything about.

6 November 2016

Liverpool find the breakthrough against Watford at Anfield. The visitors hold firm until Jordan Henderson and Philippe Coutinho's short corner routine sees the Brazilian whip in a cross from the left, and Sadio Mané directs the ball into the far corner of the net with a clever flick of his head.

12 May 2019

For once, a goal scored elsewhere is celebrated deliriously at Anfield, as news breaks that title rivals Manchester City have fallen 1-0 down to a Glenn Murray header at Brighton, putting the Reds – beating Wolves 1-0 at the time – two points clear at the top of the Premier League live table as things stand ...

28

25 May 1977

Terry McDermott races on to a pass from Steve Heighway and into the Borussia Mönchengladbach box, before hitting a left-foot shot past Wolfgang Kneib to put the Reds ahead in the 1977 European Cup Final in Rome.

2 September 1978

Liverpool go 3-0 up against Tottenham at a sun-drenched Anfield. Terry McDermott's deep cross into the box from the right flank finds Ray Kennedy, who heads the ball home after a mistake from the Spurs keeper.

14 October 1978

David Johnson puts Liverpool 1-0 up against Derby County at Anfield. Steve Heighway's cross from the right is chested down by Graeme Souness and then Kenny Dalglish takes over – but his touch, for once, is heavy, and Johnson instead races on to the loose ball before hammering a shot high into the roof of the net from eight yards.

1 April 1981

Alan Hansen powers Jimmy Case's corner towards goal and West Ham defender Billy Bonds inadvertently helps the ball on its way past his own goalkeeper, as the Reds make it two goals in three minutes in the 1981 League Cup Final replay at Villa Park.

13 April 1991

The irrepressible John Barnes is sent clear by Ian Rush, and the England winger keeps his cool to calmly slide the ball past Leeds United keeper John Lukic and put the Reds 4-0 up at Elland Road in the First Division clash.

14 December 1996

Robbie Fowler becomes the fastest Liverpool player to score 100 goals, as he puts the rampant Reds 2-0 up against struggling Middlesbrough in his 165th game for the club. Stan Collymore is denied a goal as his fierce shot strikes the foot of the Boro post, but Fowler reacts fastest to volley the rebound home from ten yards and beat Ian Rush's record.

10 March 2009

Liverpool get their second fortuitous decision of the night against Real Madrid, as a pass is played to Fabio Aurelio on the right of the Spaniards' box and as he controls it with his chest, the ball hits Gabriel Heinze's shoulder and the assistant referee flags for a penalty, which the referee awards.

Steven Gerrard makes no mistake to put the Reds 2-0 up on the night and 3-0 up on aggregate.

14 March 2009

Trailing 1-0, a long clearance upfield relieves the pressure on the Liverpool defence. Nemanja Vidic seems comfortable as the ball comes towards him, but Fernando Torres's persistence pays off, as the Manchester United defender slips, allowing Torres a clear run on goal, and the

Spaniard makes no mistake with a low shot that makes it 1-1 at Old Trafford.

14 April 2009

Liverpool's mission impossible starts to become a distinct possibility, as Xabi Alonso sends Petr Cech the wrong way from the penalty spot. Trailing 3-1 from the Champions League quarter-final first leg, the Reds double their lead at Stamford Bridge after a foul by Branislav Ivanovic to level the aggregate score with Chelsea in a pulsating all-English tie.

8 May 2012

A rampant Liverpool go 3-0 up before the half-hour mark. Jonjo Shelvey whips in a deep corner towards Andy Carroll who nods it down back into the six-yard box, where Daniel Agger stoops to head the bouncing ball past Ross Turnbull and into the roof of the net.

29

21 April 1962

Kevin Lewis scores his and Liverpool's second to put the Reds further in front against Southampton at Anfield. Lewis's first goal is a scrappy affair, but this is more emphatic. Ian Callaghan sends in a fine cross from the right and Roger Hunt powers a header towards goal, only for Saints keeper Godfrey to push the ball out – but only as far as Lewis, who heads the ball powerfully into the net to make it 2-0. That will be the end of the scoring, with the win confirming the Second Division title, and in doing so, ends Liverpool's eight-year exile from the top division.

18 April 1964

A pivotal moment as Liverpool look for the victory that will crown them First Division champions for the sixth time. Leading 1-0, Ronnie Yates handles the ball as George Eastham flicks it up and the referee awards a penalty. Eastham strikes the ball with power, but Tommy Lawrence makes a stunning save to keep the Reds in the lead.

15 August 1964

Gordon Wallace puts Liverpool ahead in the FA Charity Shield clash with West Ham United at Anfield. Ian Callaghan's clever pass just inside the full-back allows Wallace to run in behind and thump a shot in off the post to make it 1-0.

6 November 1991

Mike Marsh puts Liverpool level on aggregate against Auxerre in the UEFA Cup second round second leg at Anfield, and 2-0 ahead on the night. Good approach play involving Steve McManaman and Ray Houghton sees the latter burst into the box, before lofting a cross into the six-yard box for Marsh to power a header home and make it 2-2 overall and everything to play for.

28 August 1994

Robbie Fowler makes it two goals in two minutes as he puts Liverpool 2-0 up against Arsenal. Steve McManaman brings the ball forward with purpose before playing it left to Fowler, who momentarily pauses before hitting a low shot in off the post from the edge of the box to send Anfield wild.

16 September 1995

Already leading Blackburn Rovers 2-0 at Anfield, the ball is played to Stan Collymore 25 yards from goal, and the powerful forward sweeps a curling shot high past Tim Flowers and into the top left-hand corner with seemingly minimal effort to all but wrap the points up for the Reds.

23 February 2008

Fernando Torres, having just put Liverpool on level terms against Middlesbrough at Anfield, scores his second goal in two minutes to put the Reds 2-1 up. The Spaniard receives the ball 20 yards out and then strikes a powerful drive past the goalkeeper's right and into the back of the net.

3 February 2013

Trailing 1-0 to Edin Džeko's 23rd-minute goal, Liverpool hit back with a superb equaliser. Former City striker Daniel Sturridge receives a short past from Lucas and cracks a thunderous low shot past Joe Hart from 22 yards out to make it 1-1, but out of respect for his former employers, he doesn't celebrate his goal at the Etihad.

26 May 2018

A huge blow for Liverpool's hopes of winning the Champions League Final, as Real Madrid's Sergio Ramos clashes with Mo Salah, injuring the Egyptian's shoulder in the process. The Spaniard falls on top of Salah during a challenge and despite several minutes of treatment, the crestfallen Reds talisman is unable to continue and is helped from the pitch by the medical team.

30

26 November 1989

In the top-of-the-table First Division clash, Liverpool strike first on the half hour. Having missed the chance to go ahead through a John Barnes penalty, the Reds get the goal they deserve when Ian Rush passes the ball to Steve McMahon some 25 yards out, and he fizzes a low, right-foot shot into the bottom corner of the Arsenal net to put the Reds ahead.

20 November 1996

Robbie Fowler gives second-placed Liverpool the lead in the Anfield Merseyside derby. Having come close on a couple of occasions, the Reds finally beat Neville Southall as Jamie Redknapp whips a cross into the box and Fowler sends a bullet header into the net from six yards out to make it 1-0.

25 February 2001

Sander Westerveld's long kick up front is headed on by Emile Heskey and, instinctively, Robbie Fowler latches on to the pass and hits a half-volley over Birmingham City keeper Ian Bennett from 25 yards and into the net to put the Reds ahead in the 2001 League Cup Final at the Millennium Stadium.

18 September 2018

The Reds begin their Champions League group stage campaign at home to Paris Saint-Germain in what will be a thrilling encounter at Anfield. The Reds draw first blood as Andy Robertson whips in a superb cross and Daniel Sturridge rises to plant a header home from six yards out.

31

28 August 1994

Robbie Fowler completes the quickest Premier League hat-trick of all time as he nets his third goal against Arsenal. Having already scored two in two minutes, Fowler collects the ball inside the box from John Barnes but is initially denied by David Seaman. Fowler is first to the rebound, calmly keeping the ball in play before firing into the net from a tight angle to create club history, having bagged a treble in just four minutes and 33 seconds.

19 April 2003

With the score still 0-0 at a sunny Goodison Park, a long ball is played out to Michael Owen on the left flank. The Liverpool forward controls the ball before taking on the Toffees right-back, skipping past that and another challenge, before entering the box and firing a fierce, low, angled shot into the net to give the Reds the advantage.

6 November 2016

A second goal in three minutes for the Reds against Watford. Jordan Henderson finds Philippe Coutinho on the edge of the box, and the Brazilian controls the pass before hitting a powerful low drive past the keeper from 20 yards to make it 2-0.

4 April 2018

Liverpool complete a first-half demolition job on Manchester City in the Champions League quarter-final first leg at Anfield, as Mo Salah digs a beauty of a cross into the six-yard box, where Sadio Mané arrives to head past Ederson and make it 3-0 with barely half an hour played.

4 December 2019

Divock Origi restores Liverpool's two-goal cushion with a superb goal against Everton. Dejan Lovren plays a 50-yard pass into Origi's path, and the Belgian deftly takes the ball down and then immediately lobs the onrushing Jordan Pickford to put the Reds 3-1 up at Anfield.

32

10 May 1973

Emlyn Hughes heads the ball into the Borussia Mönchengladbach box and Bertie Vogts's attempted clearance only finds the head of John Toshack, who nods the ball down instinctively for Kevin Keegan, who gets a toe-poke on the ball to send it past the keeper and double Liverpool's lead in the 1973 UEFA Cup Final first leg.

21 August 1982

Liverpool secure the FA Charity Shield with a 1-0 win over Tottenham Hotspur at Wembley. The only goal of the game comes as Phil Thompson brings the ball forward with purpose before playing a superb pass into Ian Rush's path, and the Welsh striker takes the ball around former Liverpool legend Ray Clemence before slotting into the empty net.

16 September 1990

John Barnes and Steve McMahon again combine superbly to create a chance in the First Division Anfield clash with Manchester United. After a fine ball from Barnes, McMahon drifts past a challenge on the edge of the box before playing the ball into the path of Peter Beardsley, who calmly slots past Les Sealey for his and Liverpool's second of the afternoon.

30 August 1998

Liverpool travel to St James' Park looking to consolidate top spot in the Premier League. The travelling fans are treated to a Michael Owen masterclass in finishing and a 15-minute hat-trick – the third of which sees the teenage striker collect the ball before skipping past his marker and hitting a sumptuous right-foot shot past Shay Given to put the Reds 3-1 up with just 32 minutes on the clock.

13 January 2001

After some excellent build-up play by Liverpool, Danny Murphy lays off a pass to Steven Gerrard on the right of the Aston Villa box, and the gifted youngster immediately fires a superb shot like an arrow past the keeper from 20 yards out to double the Reds' lead at Villa Park.

13 May 2006

Trailing 2-0 to West Ham United in the 2006 FA Cup Final, Steven Gerrard picks up the ball just inside the Hammers half before lofting a sumptuous long ball into the path of Djibril Cisse, who times his run to perfection as he volleys past Shaka Hislop to halve the deficit.

21 November 2015

A quite brilliant goal puts Liverpool 3-1 up against Manchester City at the Etihad with barely half an hour played. Emre Can has his back to the City box when he plays a back-heel that plays in Philippe Coutinho, and the Brazilian plays a simple pass to Roberto Firmino who gently rolls the ball home from five yards for his first Liverpool goal.

1 April 2017

Having been pegged back to 1-1 in the Merseyside derby at Anfield, the Reds retake the lead from a goal that oozes class and quality. Philippe Coutinho moves towards the Everton box with intent, shrugs off one challenge, before shifting the ball to his right and curling a beautiful shot past the Toffees keeper to restore the Liverpool lead.

29 December 2018

What you could call a typical Liverpool goal of recent times, as Andy Robertson plays in a deep cross towards Mo Salah in the Arsenal box, and the Egyptian cleverly knocks the ball across to Sadio Mané, who makes it 3-1 as the irresistible Reds continue to torment a poor Gunners defence.

33

12 August 1989

Peter Beardsley wins the FA Charity Shield for Liverpool against First Division champions Arsenal at Wembley. Barry Venison's cross into the box finds Beardsley free in the Gunners box, and after controlling the ball, the Liverpool forward pokes the ball home for what will prove to be the only goal of the game.

1 October 1995

In a game where the main focus is Manchester United's Eric Cantona returning after a nine-month ban, Liverpool perhaps get lost in the hype in the early stages and are 1-0 down after just two minutes. As the half wears on, Steve McManaman picks out Robbie Fowler on the right of the United box, and after teeing himself up, Fowler unleashes an angled bullet of a shot that doesn't give Peter Schmeichel a hope.

22 March 2009

Liverpool double their lead against Aston Villa at Anfield, as Albert Riera chases a long ball to the edge of the Villa box, before unleashing a dipping volley that rockets into the top left-hand corner of the net to make it 2-0.

28 January 2014

Daniel Sturridge doubles Liverpool's lead in the Merseyside derby, as Philippe Coutinho plays the ball in behind the Toffees defence for Sturridge to run on to, and the Reds striker hits a sweet left-foot shot past Tim Howard to make it 2-0 and send Anfield wild.

34

4 May 1965

A superb free-kick routine sees Liverpool retake the lead against Inter Milan in the European Cup semi-final first leg at Anfield. Ian Callaghan shapes up to take the free kick from 20 yards out, but instead runs over the ball which is then played to Roger Hunt on the edge of the box. Hunt flicks the ball into the path of the now unmarked Callaghan who has continued his run, and the winger makes no mistake from close range to put the Reds 2-1 up.

23 April 1988

Liverpool claim a 17th top-flight title triumph after a narrow win over Tottenham at Anfield. Needing three points to be confirmed as First Division champions, Peter Beardsley receives the ball on the right flank, moves into the box and shimmies left, before curling a low drive into the far corner of Bobby Mimms's net for the only goal of the game. The win means the Reds are crowned champs with four games still to play and second-placed Manchester United trailing 15 points behind.

9 April 2000

Liverpool's pressure finally pays off, as Patrik Berger receives the ball on the edge of the Tottenham box, before spinning and unleashing a fierce drive past Ian Walker to make it 1-0 and put the Reds on their way to victory.

6 March 2011

Liverpool take the lead against Manchester United at Anfield after a breathtaking piece of individual brilliance from Luis Suarez. The Uruguayan looks as though he has nowhere to go when faced with two United defenders, but he spins away from both of them, before his quick feet take the ball around another challenge – then another – before taking the keeper out of the equation with a low pass across goal, where Dirk Kuyt has the simplest of tasks to prod the ball into the empty net.

2 March 2016

Adam Lallana shoots from 25 yards out, and although there doesn't seem to be any real power in the attempt, the ball still somehow ends up in the Manchester City net, as the Reds look for quick payback having lost the Capital One Cup Final a few days earlier.

11 December 2018

Needing a victory to move into the knockout phase of the Champions League, Mo Salah provides a moment of magic. The ball is played towards the Egyptian, who shrugs off a defender before tormenting another Napoli defender with lightning quick feet, and then slots a low right-foot shot past the keeper for what will prove to be the only goal of the game – and enough for round of 16 qualification.

9 February 2019

Leading 1-0 against Bournemouth at Anfield, Georginio Wijnaldum collects the ball on the corner of the Cherries

box. The Dutchman controls the pass before dinking a
superb chip over the keeper for a delightful second goal
for the Reds.

35

28 August 1971

A classic Liverpool goal of the era. Drawing 1-1 with Leicester City at Anfield, the Reds win a corner on the left. Steve Heighway sends the cross in and John Toshack rises to head the ball towards goal, and although it looks as though it will be cleared by the defender on the line, from nowhere, Kevin Keegan arrives to volley high into the net to make it 2-1.

12 April 1978

Liverpool double their lead against Borussia Mönchengladbach with a well-worked goal in the European Cup semi-final second leg at Anfield. Emlyn Hughes sends in a deep cross into the box, and Steve Heighway nods down for Kenny Dalglish to immediately hit a low shot into the bottom right-hand corner of the net from eight yards out, making it 2-0 on the night and 3-2 on aggregate.

30 April 1994

Though Jeremy Goss scores what proves to be the only goal of the game for Norwich City on 35 minutes, the goal is significant for being the last scored in front of the Kop as a terraced stand. The Liverpool fans give the most famous standing area in the world a fitting send-off, even though the Reds can't find an equaliser.

31 March 2007

Peter Crouch doubles Liverpool's lead with his second goal of the game. Fabio Aurelio has the ball on the left flank, before sending a measured cross into the Arsenal box, where Crouch arrives right on cue to send a superb header past Jens Lehmann into the top right-hand corner of the Gunners net.

4 December 2013

Luis Suarez completes a first-half hat-trick with a stunning solo goal. The Uruguayan flips the ball up past a defender before striking a sizzling half-volley past the Canaries keeper from the left-hand side of the box. It is his 50th Liverpool goal in just 86 games and also his third hat-trick against Norwich – a Premier League record.

28 January 2014

Liverpool run riot against Everton as Daniel Sturridge makes it 3-0 in the Merseyside derby at Anfield. Sturridge's pace is too much for a static Everton defensive line, and as he runs on to a lofted through-ball, the Reds striker lobs Tim Howard as he rushes off his line, and the ball bounces once before crossing the line just inside the post.

18 May 2016

Daniel Sturridge gives Liverpool the advantage in the Europa League Final against Sevilla. The Reds strike first when great work between Brazilians Roberto Firmino and Philippe Coutinho present a chance for Sturridge on the edge of the box, and he takes the keeper and defenders by surprise by curling a left-foot shot with the outside of the boot into the far corner from 18 yards out.

4 May 1974: Kevin Keegan scores a magnificent goal on 57 minutes to put the Reds 1-0 up against Newcastle United in the 1974 FA Cup Final at Wembley

25 May 1977: Terry McDermott puts the Reds ahead in the 1977 European Cup Final against Borussia Monchengladbach with 28 minutes played.

10 May 1978: Kenny Dalglish deftly chips the Bruges goalkeeper to score the only goal of the 1978 European Cup Final at Wembley.

Alan Kennedy puts Liverpool ahead in the League Cup Final against West Ham United held at Wembley Stadium, London on 14 March 1981. The game ended in a 1-1 draw after extra time.

15 May 1982: Mark Lawrenson (out of picture) managed 18 goals during his Liverpool career – this powerful header against Spurs was one of them, watched by a celebratory Kenny Dalglish.

5 April 1992: Barry Venison and John Barnes celebrate Ronnie Whelan's 116th-minute equaliser against Portsmouth in the FA Cup semi-final at Highbury.

28 August 1994: Robbie Fowler bags the second of his four-minutes and 33 seconds hat-trick against Arsenal at Anfield.

Ian Rush scores Liverpool's second goal on 58 minutes against Sunderland in the 1992 FA Cup Final at Wembley.

3 May 2006: Steven Gerrard scores an injury time equaliser against West Ham United in the 2006 FA Cup Final to make it 3-3 at the Millennium Stadium, Cardiff.

14 August 2016: Off and running! Sadio Mane marks his Liverpool debut with a stunning strike to put the Reds 4-1 up at the Emirates Stadium.

4 April 2018: Mohamed Salah gives Liverpool a crucial early lead against Manchester City in the Champions League quarter-final, first leg at Anfield.

Divock Origi completes a remarkable comeback for the Reds by scoring the fourth of the night against Barcelona in the UEFA Champions League semi-final second leg match at Anfield.

1 June 2019: Mohamed Salah puts Liverpool ahead from the penalty spot after just two minutes of the 2019 Champions League Final against Spurs.

21 December 2019: Roberto Firmino scores the extra-goal that ensures Liverpool are crowned FIFA World Club champions against Flamengo.

36

16 September 2016

He doesn't score that many goals, but when he does, they're usually pretty special – and this goal fits very nicely into Jordan Henderson's collection of breathtaking strikes. There seems little danger for the Chelsea defence when Henderson picks up the ball 25 yards from goal, but without much hesitation Henderson strikes a thunderbolt of a shot that flies into the top right-hand corner to give the Reds a 2-0 lead at Stamford Bridge.

24 April 2018

Liverpool draw first blood in the Champions League semi-final first leg with AS Roma. After missing several good chances, the Reds finally break the deadlock in spectacular style, as Mo Salah controls the ball on the corner of the Italian side's box, before unleashing a curling shot into the top left-hand corner that future Liverpool keeper Alisson Becker can't keep out, to make it 1-0.

18 September 2018

Liverpool double their lead against Paris Saint-Germain at Anfield. Georginio Wijnaldum is fouled in the box and James Milner calmly slots home to put the Reds firmly in control of their opening Champions League group stage clash.

2 October 2019

Compared with the first two goals Liverpool score against Red Bull Salzburg, this is a scruffier affair. Andy Robertson plays a short pass to Sadio Mané, who whips in a cross that Roberto Firmino heads towards goal. The keeper pushes his effort out but Mo Salah reacts first to roll the ball home from seven yards and make it 3-0.

37

12 September 1987

John Barnes scores on his Anfield debut. The England winger, signed for £900,000 from Watford, having already made a goal for John Aldridge earlier in the half, is tripped on the edge of the Oxford United box, and Peter Beardsley taps it to Barnes, who curls home a 20-yard shot to mark an impressive home debut.

13 April 1988

Liverpool double their lead against Nottingham Forest with a fine sweeping move. Peter Beardsley loses three Forest players in one swivel of the hips inside his own half, before spinning away and playing a wonderful pass into the path of John Aldridge, who deftly lifts the ball over the onrushing keeper to put the Reds 2-0 up at Anfield.

2 April 1995

There seems little danger when Steve McManaman collects the ball midway inside the Bolton Wanderers half, but the England winger races past a couple of challenges into the box before hitting a low shot that squeezes its way past keeper Keith Branagan to put the Reds 1-0 up in the 1995 League Cup Final at Wembley.

25 August 2007

Mohamed Sissoko puts Liverpool ahead away to Sunderland. Sissoko finishes off a fine team move with a smart finish from close range to put the Reds in control at the Stadium of Light, and the strike is also Liverpool's 7,000th goal in all competitions.

9 September 2017

Sadio Mané is controversially sent off on what will turn out to be a miserable day for Liverpool. Mané chases a high through-ball as Manchester City goalkeeper Ederson rushes out to head the danger clear. Mané's attempt to knock the ball over the Brazilian ends in a nasty collision that Ederson comes off the worst from. With a nasty gash on his face, Ederson is stretchered off, while Mané is shown a straight red card. The Reds go on to lose 5-0 at the Etihad Stadium.

38

31 May 1947

In an epic match that will eventually decide the title, third-placed Liverpool travel to Molineux to take on leaders Wolverhampton Wanderers, as both clubs vie for their first top-flight title since the end of World War Two. The Reds have taken the lead earlier in the game but are under the cosh from the home side – so when Albert Stubbins makes it 2-0, it gives Liverpool the vital breathing space they need. Wolves pull one back after the break thanks to Jimmy Dunn, and the Reds have keeper Cyril Sidlow to thank for a series of brave saves in the closing stages. Liverpool hang on to win 2-1, putting George Kay's side top – but Stoke City, two points behind and with a better goal average, still have one game to play. Reds fans will have to wait two agonising weeks before the Potters play their rearranged match with Sheffield United on 14 June, but with only a win enough to snatch the title away from Merseyside, Stoke are beaten 2-1 to confirm Liverpool as champions for the first time since 1923.

18 April 1964

Liverpool get a crucial second against Arsenal as Bill Shankly's men look to seal the First Division title. With the Gunners missing a penalty just nine minutes before, the Reds need some breathing space – and they get it when Peter Thompson weaves his way past two challenges before floating a cross into the box, but Ian St John skews his header and Alf Arrowsmith instead nods home from close range to make it 2-0.

14 August 1965

Willie Stevenson levels for Liverpool in the FA Charity Shield clash at Old Trafford. In front of a crowd of more than 48,000, George Best has given United the lead ten minutes earlier, but Stevenson's equaliser silences the home crowd in an entertaining game.

11 August 1979

Terry McDermott gives Liverpool the lead in the FA Charity Shield at Wembley. The dynamic midfielder collects a pass midway inside the Arsenal half, and as two defenders approach him, he unleashes a 20-yard left-foot shot that nestles in the bottom corner of the net, giving Pat Jennings no chance.

4 January 1994

Liverpool have been 3-0 down to Manchester United after just 23 minutes, before Nigel Clough starts the fightback on 25 minutes. His second goal of the game comes just 13 minutes later, as Steve Bruce's attempted clearance hits Roy Keane, and Clough again scores with a long-range effort to make it 2-3.

39

5 March 1960

Billy Liddell becomes Liverpool's oldest ever goalscorer when he puts the Reds 3-0 up against a poor Stoke City at Anfield. Liddell is aged 38 years and 55 days when he bags against the Potters in a game Liverpool eventually win 5-1.

23 March 1991

Ian Rush scores Liverpool's third away to Derby County with a typical predatory finish. John Barnes flicks the ball into Peter Beardsley from the left flank, and Beardsley spins off his marker before whipping a low cross into the near post, where Rush taps home from a couple of yards out to make it 3-1 at the Baseball Ground.

4 November 2001

Liverpool are already a goal up courtesy of Michael Owen when a free kick is awarded on the edge of the Manchester United box. Some 25 yards out and to the right of the box, Didi Hamann rolls the ball into the path of John Arne Riise, who sends a howitzer of a left-foot shot arrowing into the top left-hand corner to put the Reds 2-0 up ahead of half-time.

2 March 2003

After a spell of sustained pressure, Steven Gerrard lets fly from 25 yards and sees his shot loop over Manchester

United goalkeeper Fabian Barthez into the top right-hand corner of the net to put Liverpool ahead in the 2003 League Cup Final in Cardiff.

6 March 2011

Dirk Kuyt scores his – and Liverpool's – second goal in five minutes to put the Reds 2-0 up against Manchester United at a raucous Anfield. As the ball comes into the United box, Nani's wayward header goes back towards his own six-yard box, and Kuyt makes no mistake from close range.

26 March 2014

Relegation-threatened Sunderland's resistance finally ends as Liverpool, second in the Premier League, finally break the deadlock just before the break. After being awarded a free kick on the edge of the Black Cats box, Steven Gerrard steps forward to unleash a powerful free kick into the top right-hand corner to put the Reds on their way to a narrow 2-1 win.

40

6 December 1977

Terry McDermott scores Liverpool's second goal in the European Super Cup second leg against Hamburg. McDermott is filling in as a more central midfielder, and Ray Kennedy spots his intelligent run into the box and plays a deft chip into his path, and McDermott chests the ball down before hammering it home from eight yards out.

28 April 1990

Ian Rush brings Liverpool level just before the break after previously trailing 1-0 to Queen's Park Rangers. The Reds, who can win the title with a win and if Aston Villa fail to win, need one more goal to seal an 18th top-flight triumph.

23 December 1995

Liverpool are trailing to Ian Wright's early goal against Arsenal at Anfield, but five minutes before the break, the prolific Robbie Fowler equalises as he picks up Stan Collymore's flick, before cutting inside and lashing a powerful rising shot past David Seaman to make it 1-1. Fowler goes on to add two more to his tally after the break in a 3-1 victory for the Reds.

6 May 1998

Skipper Paul Ince is inspirational against Arsenal, with his two goals already putting the Reds firmly in command.

And when a corner comes in, who else but Ince climbs highest to knock it towards the angle of the six-yard box, where Michael Owen is waiting to spin and tuck a low drive past Alex Manninger and make it 3-0 before the break.

31 March 2001

Liverpool put a slight dent in Manchester United's inevitable surge towards the Premier League title with a 2-0 victory at Anfield. Already leading through Steven Gerrard's howitzer, Robbie Fowler doubles the Reds' lead just before the break, as Gerrard floats a ball into the United box, where Gary Neville slips and Fowler then has time to bring the ball down before thumping a half-volley past Fabien Barthez, as the Reds complete a league double over United for the first time in 22 years.

25 January 2012

Steven Gerrard scores against Manchester City to make it 1-1 in the Capital One Cup semi-final second leg. Daniel Agger's shot appears to strike the arm of Micah Richards as the City defender attempts to block the shot, and the referee awards a spot kick. Gerrard confidently tucks away the penalty to restore the Reds' aggregate lead.

15 December 2013

Jordan Henderson puts Liverpool 2-0 up at White Hart Lane. A long ball to Philippe Coutinho sees the Brazilian cushion a pass into Henderson's path, but his shot is saved by Hugo Lloris, as is Luis Suarez's follow-up, but Lloris can only claw the ball into Henderson's path and he makes no mistake at the second attempt.

41

5 May 1996

Ian Rush scores his last goal for Liverpool. The Welsh legend hits a crisp 22-yard shot past Eike Immel to double the Reds' lead against Manchester City, who need a win to have any chance of avoiding relegation. The game will end 2-2, but it's not enough to save City, who need to better the results of Southampton and Coventry – who also draw that day.

16 May 2001

Liverpool regain command of the UEFA Cup Final against Alavés. Dietmar Hamann spots the run of Michael Owen and threads a ball into his path. As the Alaves keeper races out of his area, Owen skips around him before being pulled down from behind just inside the box by the desperate goalkeeper. Gary McAllister is cool as a cucumber as he slots the penalty home to make it 3-1.

28 November 2004

Liverpool strike first against title-chasing Arsenal at Anfield.

With the score 0-0, Steven Gerrard strokes a pass into the path of Xabi Alonso, and the Spaniard thumps the ball past Jens Lehmann into the roof of the net from 18 yards to put the Reds a goal up.

2 March 2016

James Milner puts Liverpool 2-0 up against Manchester City at Anfield. A smart move down the right flank sees Roberto Firmino cut inside and pick out the run of Milner, who collects the pass before prodding home from ten yards out.

42

21 September 1996

Liverpool double their lead in the top-of-the-table clash with Chelsea at Anfield.

Dominic Matteo wins possession back in the centre circle and drives forward – as two Chelsea defenders converge, he plays the ball to Patrik Berger, who looks marginally offside, but the Czech midfielder doesn't hesitate, moving into the box and around the keeper before slotting home to make it 2-0 – much to the chagrin of the Chelsea players who are convinced the flag should be raised.

5 April 2008

Peter Crouch gives Liverpool the lead at the Emirates Stadium with a fine finish. Yossi Benayoun hooks the ball into Crouch's path, and the lanky striker takes the ball down, shifts to his right, and then fires a low shot home from the edge of the box.

21 December 2008

Chasing a long ball forward, Robbie Keane gets in behind the Arsenal defence before lashing an unstoppable half-volley past Manuel Almunia to level the scores at the Emirates Stadium, and silence the jeering home fans, who haven't forgotten Keane's association with Spurs!

10 December 2017

With the Merseyside derby still goalless coming up to half-time, Mo Salah shrugs off the challenge of Cuco Martina, before drifting past one challenge and sending a rising, curling shot high into the top left-hand corner of the Toffees net to put the Reds 1-0 up at Anfield.

43

19 August 1992

Ronnie Whelan lofts a pass to the left edge of the Sheffield United box where Mark Walters controls, cuts inside and then fires a low shot into the bottom corner of the net from 20 yards to put the Reds on level terms – it is also Liverpool's first ever Premier League goal.

17 December 2000

Liverpool win a free kick on the edge of the box against Manchester United at Old Trafford. Facing the Stretford End, Danny Murphy and Nick Barmby stand over the ball, before Barmby runs on and Murphy strikes a sweet curling drive that gives Fabien Barthez no chance. It will prove to be the only goal of the game.

20 April 2016

With Everton holding firm in the Merseyside derby at Anfield, James Milner shifts the ball on to his left foot near the corner flag before sending a fine cross into the six-yard box, where Divock Origi climbs highest to nod the ball home and put the Reds 1-0 up.

6 November 2016

Emre Can makes it two goals in two games as he puts Liverpool 3-0 up against Watford. It's the Reds' third goal in 16 minutes as the Hornets begin to capitulate, and it comes as Adam Lallana spots the German's drive into the box and sends in a cross that Can doesn't have to break stride for, as he nods home from close range.

30 October 2019

Liverpool pull one back against Arsenal in the Carabao Cup at Anfield. The Gunners have come back from a goal down to lead 3-1, before Harvey Elliott is brought down in the box by Martinelli, and James Milner keeps his cool to send the keeper the wrong way and make it 2-3 in the visitors' favour.

44

17 November 1973

Peter Cormack restores Liverpool's two-goal advantage just before half-time. After Steve Heighway is brought down on the left of the Ipswich Town box, Alex Lindsay chips the ball into the centre, where John Toshack rises to head towards the six-yard box, and Cormack lashes home a volley from close range to make it 3-1.

16 September 1990

A cross from the right finds Steve Nicol's run into the Manchester United box, but the Scotland international's volley loops into the air, where John Barnes rises to head the ball back across the six-yard box and past keeper Les Sealey to put the Reds 3-0 up at the break in the First Division clash.

18 October 1992

Ian Rush writes himself into Liverpool's record books as he doubles the Reds' lead at Old Trafford, and in doing so, surpasses Roger Hunt's tally to become the club's top scorer of all time. His goal against Manchester United is his 287th for the club.

4 September 2010

Jamie Carragher scores from the penalty spot against Everton to put Liverpool 2-0 up at Anfield in his testimonial match. Almost 36,000 turn out to pay tribute to one of the club's most loyal servants, and the Reds go on to win 4-1.

23 September 1986

Steve McMahon scores Liverpool's fourth goal of the evening to put the Reds 4-0 up just before the break against Fulham in the Littlewoods Cup. McMahon goes on to score four times during a 10-0 annihilation of the Cottagers, who at least have a second leg at Craven Cottage to try to turn things around!

18 October 1992

Already a goal up at Old Trafford, a struggling Liverpool go 2-0 up against Manchester United. Ronnie Rosenthal wriggles into the United box past two challenges, before pulling the ball back for Ian Rush to prod home from six yards just before the break.

13 March 1994

Liverpool fight back from a goal down to go in at the break 2-1 up and eventually win the game. The winner comes when John Barnes nonchalantly plays Robbie Fowler in behind the Everton defence, and the young Reds striker does the rest, firing an angled left-foot shot home past Neville Southall to send the Kop wild.

7 November 2010

Fernando Torres has already put Liverpool 1-0 up against Premier League leaders Chelsea, but it is the Spaniard's second goal a minute before half-time that proves most memorable. He edges into the Chelsea box from the left, waits for Ivanovic to commit himself, before nudging the ball to his right and cracking a curling powerful shot past Petr Cech to double the Reds' lead.

45

23 August 1999

Titi Camara attempts to put Patrik Berger clear in the Leeds United box, but the ball comes straight back to him, and Camara's instinctive curling shot gives the Leeds keeper no chance to make the score 1-1 at Elland Road on the stroke of half-time.

24 August 2001

There seems little danger when Emile Heskey collects a short pass midway inside the Bayern Munich half, but the Liverpool striker heads towards goal and drives between two defenders, before drawing the keeper off his line and deftly sending a left-foot shot over his dive to put the Reds in full control of the European Super Cup clash in Monaco.

4 October 2014

Adam Lallana starts and finishes a move that puts Liverpool ahead against West Bromwich Albion. The former Southampton star out-skills a Baggies defender before moving towards the penalty area, playing a one-two with Jordan Henderson, and driving a low shot past Ben Foster to make it 1-0 for the Reds.

1 May 2017

Liverpool finally get the breakthrough they need in spectacular style. Lucas Leiva dinks a ball towards the edge of the Watford box – there seems little danger as the ball falls to Emre Can, but the German midfielder spectacularly volleys an overhead kick from 18 yards that gives Hornets keeper Gomes no chance – a sublime goal that also turns out to be the winner at Vicarage Road.

24 April 2018

Liverpool double their lead against AS Roma in the Champions League semi-final first leg at Anfield. The Reds counter-attack at speed, and Roberto Firmino plays Mo Salah clear, and the Egyptian calmly clips the ball over Alisson and into the net from 18 yards out right on half-time to make it 2-0.

4 December 2019

Liverpool go 4-1 up just before half-time with a wonderful counter-attacking goal. Trent Alexander-Arnold sprints from his own half towards the Everton box, before laying the ball to his right for Sadio Mané to fire a measured low shot past Jordan Pickford to all but settle the Merseyside derby before the half-time whistle has even been blown.

45+1

19 April 2001

Liverpool are awarded a penalty after a Gary McAllister corner is inexplicably handled by Barcelona's Patrick Kluivert. With the Reds claiming a 0-0 draw in the first leg at the Camp Nou, McAllister steps up to take the spot kick, and sends Pepe Reina the wrong way and makes it 1-0 – and the goal is enough to book a place in the 2001 UEFA Cup Final.

14 August 2016

In a thrilling opening day clash at the Emirates Stadium, Liverpool equalise in first-half added time. Rob Holding's foul on Philippe Coutinho 30 yards from goal earns the Reds a free kick, and gives Coutinho the opportunity to show his ability from set-piece situations. Of course, he doesn't disappoint, sending a powerful, curling shot that gives Petr Cech no chance.

45+2

21 September 1996

Liverpool go 3-0 up against Chelsea at Anfield. The previously unbeaten West London side shoot themselves in the foot, as Stig Inge Bjørnbye's deep cross finds the head of Chelsea defender Andy Myers, but instead of clearing the danger, he attempts to guide the ball back to the keeper, but there is too much power and he only succeeds in heading it into his own net with what would otherwise be an impressive finish!

20 April 2016

Having held out for 43 minutes at Anfield, Everton concede a second goal in four minutes. Adam Lallana plays a pass to James Milner, this time on the left flank, and the Reds midfielder crosses into the middle for Mamadou Sakho to head home and put Liverpool 2-0 up.

45+3

31 October 2015

Though Jose Mourinho's Chelsea have taken an early lead, the struggling Londoners are eventually overpowered by the Reds. The equaliser comes in first-half stoppage time and is quintessential Philippe Coutinho, with the Brazilian bamboozling his marker on the edge of the box, before cutting in from the left and curling a sumptuous shot into the top left corner of Asmir Begovic's net.

46

17 August 1964

Having set up Gordon Wallace for Liverpool's first goal in European competition against Knattspyrnufélag Reykjavíkur, Roger Hunt doubles the Reds' lead in Iceland. This time, Wallace returns the favour by setting up Hunt on the edge of the six-yard box and, despite the attention of five home defenders, he outmuscles his markers to put the ball in the back of the net.

3 April 1974

Liverpool make the breakthrough just after the restart in the FA Cup semi-final replay with Leicester City at Villa Park. Having drawn the first game at Old Trafford 0-0 just four days earlier, both teams again can't be separated after a goalless first 45. But Steve Heighway's persistence on the left and cross into the middle causes an almighty scramble that sees a clearance off the line hit Brian Hall and go into the net to put the Reds 1-0 up.

24 August 2001

Just 13 seconds after the second half of the European Super Cup begins, Liverpool add a third to their tally against Bayern Munich. A long ball from defence sees Michael Owen get in behind the Bayern defence, and the young striker then puts an angled shot past German legend Oliver Kahn to put the Reds firmly in control and 3-0 up.

30 January 2007

Dirk Kuyt puts Liverpool ahead at Upton Park with a stunning strike. With the score 0-0, the ball falls to the Dutchman 20 yards out, and his howitzer of a shot thumps the underside of the bar before bouncing down and back high up into the roof of the net.

19 January 2019

A pumped Crystal Palace are having a real go at Anfield and have led 1-0 at the break, before the Reds grab a large slice of luck – and it won't be the only fortuitous moment in this game. Liverpool storm out of the blocks against the Eagles after the restart, and when Virgil van Dijk's long-range shot hits James McArthur and balloons up, it is Mo Salah who is quickest to react, volleying the ball in from close range to make it 1-1.

47

23 April 1973

Liverpool know that victory against a Leeds United side also still with a chance of winning the title will secure the championship. With the Reds' goal difference far superior to second-placed Arsenal, victory will mean the Gunners will need to win their last game by 12 goals. Leeds, with two games in hand, will move within four points with victory and, with a comparable goal difference, will be in with a great chance of taking the title themselves. Peter Cormack, however, dramatically swings the advantage the Reds' way, as he strikes a low shot past David Harvey from close range, after great work by Kevin Keegan, to make it 1-0 in front of the Kop.

7 November 1981

Liverpool break the deadlock against Everton in the 125th league Merseyside derby at Anfield. With the Toffees giving away a cheap corner after a throw-in to the keeper crosses the byeline, a deep cross into the box finds Ronnie Whelan on the edge of the box, and his first-time volley is saved by Jim Arnold, but Kenny Dalglish is first to the loose ball and fires a shot high into the net to put the Reds 1-0 up.

23 March 1991

Liverpool all but finish off Derby County with a goal straight after the restart. Peter Beardsley is the architect, driving forward on the left before playing a pinpoint pass to John Barnes, who then unleashes a powerful low shot past Peter Shilton to put the Reds 4-1 up and firmly in the driving seat.

9 May 1992

After a goalless first half at Wembley, Steve McManaman wriggles down the right flank before playing a clever pass into the feet of Michael Thomas, who hits a spectacular half-volley into the top left-hand corner of the net from 12 yards out to put Liverpool a goal to the good in the 1992 FA Cup Final against Sunderland.

5 October 1993

An 18-year-old Robbie Fowler completes his hat-trick against Fulham with only 47 minutes played. Don Hutchison brings the ball forward before playing in Rob Jones, who gets to the byline before squaring into the middle, where Fowler makes no mistake from close range.

8 December 2004

Needing to win the final Champions League group stage match against Olympiacos by a margin of two goals, the Reds go into the break trailing 1-0 and needing three to progress. On one of those special Anfield nights, the comeback begins when Harry Kewell gets to the byline before crossing low into the middle, where sub Florent Sinama-Pongolle prods home from close range. Game on!

28 December 2005

Leading 2-1 against Everton at Goodison Park, the ball is played to Djibril Cisse on the left flank, and the Reds forward heads towards the box. A clever shimmy takes him past a defender, before firing an angled, measured low shot home to make it 3-1.

10 March 2009

If the first two goals have been questionable from Real Madrid's point of view, there is no doubt about the Reds' third, which is simply sublime. Ryan Babel's run and cross in from the left finds Steven Gerrard, who adjusts to guide a controlled volley into the roof of the net to give Iker Casillas no chance, and put Liverpool 3-0 up at Anfield and 4-0 ahead on aggregate.

48

30 April 1966

Needing a victory to seal Bill Shankly's second First Division title as manager, Liverpool take on Chelsea in the penultimate game of the season. The teams are locked at 0-0 at the break, with tension at Anfield high – but just three minutes after the restart, the Reds are ahead. Gerry Byrne plays a through-ball for Roger Hunt, and the club legend manages to just keep the ball in play with a low cross towards goal that keeper John Dunn appears to deflect into his own net. Hunt was credited with the goal and the Kop didn't care either way!

2 September 1978

David Johnson makes it 4-0 for Liverpool against Tottenham. Johnson is involved in a fine team move that ends with Kenny Dalglish seeing a low shot towards goal saved by the keeper, but Johnson is on hand to drill the ball home from eight yards out.

14 April 2016

Trailing 2-0 from two early Borussia Dortmund goals and 3-1 down on aggregate, Liverpool begin to claw their way back into the Europa League quarter-final tie. As the Reds attack the Kop, Emre Can plays a perfectly weighted pass into the path of Divock Origi, who finishes with a low drive past the keeper from the edge of the box.

49

16 November 1946

Jack Balmer completes an incredible six-minute hat-trick to put the Reds 3-0 up against Derby County at the Baseball Ground. Balmer scores in the 43rd and 46th minutes, and his third makes it back-to-back hat-tricks for the prolific striker. He will add a fourth just 11 minutes later in a 4-1 victory.

15 August 1964

Ian Callaghan and Gordon Wallace exchange passes midway inside the West Ham United half in the FA Charity Shield clash at Anfield. A pass is then played to full-back Gerry Byrne, who carries the ball forward 15 yards before smashing a shot past the keeper from distance to put Liverpool 2-1 up. The Hammers will snatch a late equaliser through Geoff Hurst, and the shield is shared between the clubs for a season – something the Reds will make a habit of in the coming years!

21 September 1996

Patrik Berger scores Liverpool's third goal in seven minutes and fourth overall as Chelsea capitulate at Anfield. Dennis Wise is pickpocketed on the halfway line by Steve McManaman, who prods the ball into the path of Berger, who races clear before tucking in his second of the afternoon to make it 4-0.

21 April 2009

Liverpool equalise in what will be a remarkable game against Arsenal at Anfield. Trailing 1-0, Dirk Kuyt gets to the corner of the Gunners box before crossing into the middle, where Fernando Torres rises to head the ball into the bottom right-hand corner.

1 January 2011

Trailing 1-0 at half-time to Bolton Wanderers, Liverpool fight back after the break, and it's a goal of real quality that levels the score. The ball is played to David N'Gog, who cushions a pass to Steven Gerrard, who immediately dispatches a pinpoint cross into the Bolton box for Fernando Torres to volley home the leveller. A sumptuous team goal.

14 August 2016

Liverpool come from behind to lead 2-1 at the Emirates Stadium against Arsenal. A fine team move involving Roberto Firmino, Philippe Coutinho and Georginio Wijnaldum sees the latter find Adam Lallana in the Gunners box, and after shifting the ball to the right, Lallana fires a low shot past the keeper.

23 November 2019

Sadio Mané bags his tenth of the season as Liverpool finally break down a spirited Crystal Palace at Selhurst Park. The hosts, who have seen a goal controversially chalked off by VAR in the first half, are punished when Andy Robertson finds Mané, who makes no mistake with a low shot from just inside the box.

50

14 April 1976

Phil Thompson puts the Reds ahead at Anfield in the UEFA Cup semi-final second leg against Barcelona. After a magnificent 1-0 win in Catalonia, Thompson's goal doubles Liverpool's aggregate lead, and although Barça level two minutes later, there are no further goals and the Reds book their place in the final.

14 August 1976

The telepathic duo that is Kevin Keegan and John Toshack combine superbly to give Liverpool the lead in the FA Charity Shield at Wembley. Keegan heads a lofted pass down to Toshack on the edge of the Southampton box, and the Welshman fires a low shot to the left of Ian Turner and into the back of the net for what proves to be the only goal of the game.

6 March 1993

Having come off the bench just before the break, Ian Rush equalises against Manchester United in a tense Anfield clash. As the ball is played to Rush, he holds off the challenge of Steve Bruce, before lifting a shot up and over Peter Schmeichel to level the scores and send Anfield wild.

17 March 2018

As snow falls at Anfield, so does Watford's porous defence, with Mo Salah the destroyer-in-chief. The

Egyptian's double strike has already put the Reds in total control, and it is Salah who crosses for Roberto Firmino to cleverly flick the ball home from close range not long after the restart to put Liverpool 3-0 up and on their way to a 5-0 win.

22 January 2011

Having lost 1-0 to Wolves just a month before, Liverpool are keen to gain revenge quickly at Molineux. Already a goal to the good at the break, the Reds double their advantage through a stunning strike. A headed clearance falls to Raul Meireles 25 yards out, and he hits the ball first time on the volley with power, giving the keeper no chance.

17 February 2013

Though Liverpool end up beating Swansea City 5-0 at Anfield, it is the third goal that is the pick of the bunch, as Jose Enrique starts the move before Daniel Sturridge and Luis Suarez exchange passes, and Enrique finishes off the attack by firing in emphatically from six yards out.

28 January 2014

On a wonderful day at Anfield Luis Suarez caps off a memorable Merseyside derby by putting the Reds 4-0 up with 40 minutes still to play. Suarez nips in ahead of two Everton defenders on the halfway line, before heading towards goal chased by two Toffees players. He keeps his cool as he enters the box, before expertly tucking a low shot past Tim Howard for what will be the final goal of the game.

51

14 April 2019

Liverpool finally get the goal they need against Chelsea in a tricky Premier League encounter at Anfield. Jordan Henderson is the architect as he takes the ball wide and right of the box, before lifting a cross towards the back post, where Sadio Mané rises to nod home in front of the Kop and makes it 1-0.

10 November 2019

In a crucial Premier League clash with Manchester City, Sadio Mané puts Liverpool firmly in the driving seat just after the break. Skipper Jordan Henderson manages to get to the byline, before whipping a cross into the six-yard box for Mané to head past Claudio Bravo and put the Reds 3-0 up against the reigning champions.

52

21 May 1977

Liverpool take on Manchester United at Wembley in the FA Cup Final, and all three goals come within the space of five frantic minutes. United have gone ahead on 51 minutes, but Joey Jones finds Jimmy Case on the edge of the United box a minute later, and the Liverpool midfielder controls the ball, tees himself up, before spinning around and firing a shot into the top right-hand corner. Unfortunately, United score again on 55 minutes and win the game 2-1, denying Bob Paisley's side an unprecedented treble.

7 November 1981

Liverpool double their lead against Everton with Kenny Dalglish's second goal in five minutes. Terry McDermott is the architect as he plays a superb first-time pass with the outside of his right boot to send Dalglish clear on the left of the box, and the Scot makes no mistake with a measured low finish into the bottom right corner of the net to make it 2-0 and send the Kop wild.

6 November 1982

Alan Hansen is again the architect, as the classy Scot brings the ball out of defence before passing to Ian Rush, who hits a low shot from 20 yards that takes a deflection before beating Neville Southall to put Liverpool 2-0 up at Goodison Park. It is the Welsh striker's second of the afternoon – but things will only get better for the Reds frontman.

18 August 1990

John Barnes wins and converts the penalty that sees Liverpool share the FA Charity Shield with Manchester United at Wembley. United lead 1-0 at the break, but Barnes is felled by Gary Pallister, and the England winger makes no mistake from the spot.

1 October 1995

Liverpool go 2-1 up at Old Trafford with a goal that silences the home support who, against any other side, would probably begrudgingly applaud. Michael Thomas's pass is chased by Robbie Fowler and Gary Neville, and the Liverpool striker shoulder-charges Neville off the ball, before heading just inside the box and impudently chipping Peter Schmeichel at the Stretford End.

15 September 2001

With Everton searching for an equaliser at 2-1 down, Liverpool clear a cross out of the box and counter-attack. The ball is played to John Arne Riise still in his own half, and the Norwegian left-back races forward, before tormenting the Everton right-back and then drilling home a low shot to make it 3-1 at Goodison Park.

27 October 2019

Despite going behind after 45 seconds to a Harry Kane goal and seeing Son Heung-Min hit the bar – not to mention the visitors missing at least two more gilt-edged chances – Liverpool hit back to level the score. Fabinho's chip into the Spurs box finds Jordan Henderson, who hits a low shot into the ground and past Gazzaniga from the corner of the six-yard box to make it 1-1 and leave Spurs scratching their heads.

53

18 April 1964

Liverpool have one hand on the title as Peter Thompson makes it 3-0 against Arsenal at Anfield. Thompson cuts in from the left before striking a right-foot shot that gives former Reds keeper Furnell no chance – much to the delight of the Anfield crowd, who give Thompson a standing ovation for his effort.

25 May 2005

Steven Gerrard pulls a goal back as Liverpool finally spark into life in the Champions League Final in Istanbul. Having trailed 3-0 to AC Milan at the break, Gerrard's goal comes at the perfect time, with the skipper rising to head home John Arne Riise's cross to give the Reds a lifeline in a game that seems as good as over at half-time.

11 November 2018

With lowly Fulham just about hanging on at 1-0 down, Xherdan Shaqiri all but seals the points. Andy Robertson drives down the left flank before spotting the Swiss international's run towards the box, and the Scot's deep cross is perfect for Shaqiri to calmly volley home from six yards to put the Reds in total control.

19 January 2019

Having levelled just after the restart through Mo Salah, another of the Reds' Three Musketeers puts Liverpool

2-1 up against Crystal Palace. Naby Keita finds Roberto Firmino in the box, and the Brazilian turns his marker before firing a low shot into the bottom right corner.

14 April 2019

Having finally broken Chelsea's resistance with a Sadio Mané goal just after the restart, Mo Salah puts the game firmly in the Reds' control as he drifts in from the right flank, before hitting a howitzer of a shot into the top left-hand corner of the Chelsea net. A truly stunning goal from the Egyptian.

54

30 April 2005

Trailing to an early Middlesbrough goal at Anfield, the ball is played to Steven Gerrard some 30 yards-plus from goal. The Reds skipper controls the pass, waits for it to bounce, before slicing a curling, unstoppable left-foot volley into the top left-hand corner at the Kop end.

13 May 2006

Steven Gerrard thunders home an unstoppable rising shot from just inside the West Ham box to put the Reds level at 2-2 in the 2006 FA Cup Final, to send half of the Millennium Stadium in Cardiff wild.

21 March 2012

With the score locked at 0-0 against Queen's Park Rangers at Loftus Road, Sebastian Coates spectacularly puts Liverpool ahead. Stewart Downing's low cross is cleared by Bobby Zamora, but only as far as the lurking Coates, who acrobatically volleys home from eight yards.

7 May 2019

The Liverpool fans start to believe, as Georginio Wijnaldum makes it 2-0 for the Reds against Barcelona. Trent Alexander-Arnold's low cross into the box doesn't seem to be heading towards a Liverpool shirt, but Wijnaldum makes the ball his as he arrives to sweep a low shot past ter Stegen and put Liverpool within sight of the Catalans at 2-3 on aggregate.

55

14 August 1971

Emlyn Hughes gets a deflection on a rasping Tommy Smith drive to put Liverpool 3-1 up against Nottingham Forest at Anfield. The game is best remembered for the stunning debut by new signing Kevin Keegan.

6 December 1977

An increasingly confident Terry McDermott scores his second of the night to put Liverpool 3-0 up in the second leg of the European Super Cup against Hamburg. Allowed acres of space to run towards the Hamburg box, McDermott unleashes a 20-yard howitzer into the top right-hand corner to the delight of Anfield and his team-mates.

14 October 1978

Ray Kennedy nods home to put the Reds 2-0 up against Derby Country at Anfield. Jimmy Case receives the ball on the right, just inside the Derby half, before sending a deep cross towards the Rams box, and Kennedy heads the ball over the keeper as he comes off his line.

6 November 1982

Mark Lawrenson puts Liverpool 3-0 up at Goodison Park in what will be the most prolific scoring campaign of his career. A throw-in finds Kenny Dalglish, who leaves his marker for dust, and the silky Scot sends a measured cross into the six-yard box for Lawrenson to prod home. Lawro will go on to bag seven goals for the Reds that season.

5 October 1993

Robbie Fowler scores his fourth of the evening to put Liverpool 4-0 up against Fulham in the League Cup. Jamie Redknapp spots Julian Dicks's run down the left, and his fine cross is headed home by the teenage Fowler from six yards out.

19 May 2001

Looking to secure third spot and Champions League football on the final day of the 2000/01 campaign, the Reds struggle to break down a stubborn mid-table Charlton Athletic at The Valley. It seems it will take something special to find the breakthrough – and Robbie Fowler provides it. As a corner comes in, Addicks keeper Sasa Ilic flaps at the ball, which falls to Fowler, who, with his back to goal, hooks it back over his head, over Ilic and a defender on the line to put his team on their way to a 4-0 win.

23 January 2016

Having led 1-0, the Reds find themselves 3-1 down against Norwich City at Carrow Road, until Jordan Henderson starts an amazing comeback by making it 3-2. The Liverpool skipper sweeps home a cross from the right from ten yards out, and suddenly, it's game on again!

26 May 2018

James Milner's deep corner finds the head of Dejan Lovren, who heads into the six-yard box where Sadio Mané is fastest to react, toe-poking the ball past Keylor Navas to bring the Reds level against Real Madrid in the 2018 Champions League Final in Kyiv.

56

4 November 1961

The first goal from a player that will become a genuine Liverpool legend. Ian Callaghan puts Liverpool 2-0 up away to Preston North End. The 19-year-old midfielder goes on to play more than 850 games for the Reds, during a 21-year stay at Anfield. This goal is his first of 68 strikes for Liverpool, and helps his side to a 3-1 win at Deepdale.

6 December 1977

Terry McDermott completes a magnificent hat-trick with his second goal in two minutes in the second leg of the European Super Cup. Ray Kennedy drives into the Hamburg half before playing the ball to McDermott, and his low shot gives the keeper no chance and makes it 4-0 on the night. It caps a display that leads to McDermott becoming first choice as an attacking central midfielder, after previously playing wider roles in the team.

12 April 1978

Jimmy Case sends Anfield wild as he puts Liverpool 3-0 up against Borussia Mönchengladbach. Ray Kennedy finds Case on the right of the Germans' box, and Case cuts inside of a defender before unleashing one of his trademark cannonball shots that flies past the keeper and into the roof of the net to put the Reds firmly on course for the European Cup Final.

2 September 1978

Kenny Dalglish is the creator of Liverpool's fifth of the afternoon against Tottenham, as he slips a pass into the path of David Johnson, who fires a low shot through the keeper's legs from 18 yards out to the delight of the Anfield crowd.

10 May 1986

Trailing 1-0 in the FA Cup Final, Jan Mølby splits the Everton defence with a slide-rule pass, as Ian Rush darts into the box, takes the ball around Neville Southall, before sliding the ball into the empty net to make it 1-1 and send one half of Wembley wild.

23 March 1991

Liverpool increase their lead of Derby County to 5-1. There is more than a shade of luck involved as John Barnes looks for alternatives, before laying the ball towards the edge of the box where Steve Nicol arrives, and the Scot hits a low shot that takes one, possibly two, deflections on its way into the back of the net, leaving Peter Shilton stranded.

30 November 1997

A goal worthy of winning any game. Liverpool win a throw-in in Arsenal's final third, and the ball is thrown to Steve McManaman, who lets it bounce once before unleashing an unstoppable shot into the top corner from just outside the left of the Gunners box.

25 May 2005

Vladimir Smicer's harmless-looking 25-yard shot is fumbled by Milan keeper Dida, as Liverpool make it two goals in two minutes in the 2005 Champions League Final to send more than 20,000 Liverpool fans inside the Ataturk Stadium in Istanbul crazy. Rafa Benitez's men still trail 3-2, but suddenly what looks an impossible task is on again as the Reds turn the game on its head.

21 April 2009

Liverpool go 2-1 up against Arsenal and Dirk Kuyt is again the provider. The Dutch forward whips a tempting ball into the six-yard box and Yossi Benayoun sees his header clawed out by Lucasz Fabianski – but the referee indicates the ball has crossed the line and awards the goal.

14 August 2016

A swashbuckling run down the right flank sees Nathaniel Clyne whip a low cross into the Arsenal box, and Philippe Coutinho flicks the ball home from close range to put the Reds 3-1 up on the opening-day clash at the Emirates.

10 September 2016

Already leading Leicester City 2-1 at Anfield, Adam Lallana receives the ball on the right side of the Foxes box, and immediately hits a howitzer of a shot across and into the top left-hand corner to make it 3-1 for the Reds.

10 April 2018

With Manchester City trailing 3-0 from the first leg but 1-0 up and looking for a second goal in the Champions

League quarter-final second leg at the Etihad, Sadio Mané breaks into the City box only to be denied by Ederson, but as the ball spills free, Mo Salah quickly takes it to the left before chipping the ball over Nicolas Otamendi and into the back of the net to put the Reds 4-1 up on aggregate.

24 April 2018

Sadio Mané puts Liverpool 3-0 up against AS Roma in the Champions League semi-final first leg. Mo Salah, scorer of the first two goals, finds Mané with a low cross, and the Senegalese striker sweeps the ball home from close range.

7 May 2019

Georginio Wijnaldum completes the most incredible 122 seconds of his career as he rises to head Liverpool's third against Barcelona and make the aggregate score 3-3 on the night. Xherdan Shaqiri whips a ball in from the left and Wijnaldum rises between two static Barça defenders to send a powerful header past ter Stegen for his second goal in two unforgettable minutes.

57

25 April 1914

Liverpool's first ever FA Cup Final ends when Bertie Freeman bags a 57th-minute winner for Burnley. The game, played at Crystal Palace in London (with Wembley not constructed until 1923), attracts more than 72,000 fans, as the Clarets hold on to win 1-0.

18 April 1964

The outstanding Peter Thompson all but seals the title for Liverpool in style with a long-range effort that puts the Reds 4-0 up against Arsenal. Thompson, who has scored just minutes before, drifts in from the wing to hit a howitzer from distance that gives the unsighted Furnell no chance and sends Anfield into raptures as a result.

17 August 1964

Liverpool's first European Cup tie – a preliminary round first leg away to Icelandic amateurs Knattspyrnufélag Reykjavíkur – keeps getting better, as Phil Chisnall makes it 3-0 after good work from Ian Callaghan.

4 May 1974

With the score 0-0 in the 1974 FA Cup Final, Tommy Smith crosses into the Newcastle United box, and Kevin Keegan volleys Liverpool in front as the Reds look to win the trophy for only the second time.

21 September 1996

Liverpool go 5-0 up against Chelsea at Anfield with more than a shade of luck going the Reds' way for the third time in the game. Having already had a controversial second goal allowed despite looking possibly offside, then a bizarre own goal going in, John Barnes strikes a volley from 18 yards out that takes a wicked deflection and wrong-foots the Chelsea keeper. Game over.

18 April 2007

Steven Gerrard takes the game by the scruff of the neck to earn Liverpool three points. Against a decidedly average Middlesbrough side, the Reds are far from their best until Gerrard decides to take matters into his own hands, and, from typical Gerrard territory, he drives forward towards the Boro box before unleashing a 25-yard special to make it 1-0.

2 March 2016

Liverpool cut through Manchester City's defence like a knife through butter, as first Divock Origi holds up the ball for Adam Lallana, who then heads towards the City box before playing in Firmino, who strikes a low shot past Joe Hart to make it 3-0 on the night.

6 November 2016

Liverpool go 4-0 up, with Roberto Firmino tapping home from close range. Adam Lallana gets to the byline far too easily and his low cross finds Firmino, who has the simplest of tasks to seal the points with less than an hour played.

4 November 2017

Liverpool restore a two-goal lead over West Ham United at the London Stadium. Having just conceded a goal to the hosts, the Reds break forward and Roberto Firmino plays in Alex Oxlade-Chamberlain on the right of the box – his first shot is saved by Joe Hart but goes back to Oxlade-Chamberlain, who makes no mistake at the second attempt.

10 December 2019

A vital goal for the Reds. Needing to avoid defeat against Red Bull Salzburg in the final Champions League group stage game in Austria, Liverpool finally break the deadlock. Andy Robertson plays a pass into midfield from the left flank, and Sadio Mané drives past one challenge into the box, and as the keeper races out towards him, he crosses into the centre, where Naby Keita rises to head the ball between three defenders and into the net to make it 1-0.

58

28 December 1959

Alan A'Court becomes the first Liverpool player to score a goal under the leadership of Bill Shankly. The new boss has seen his charges beaten 4-0 against Cardiff and 3-0 against Charlton Athletic on Boxing Day – but A'Court heads home a Tommy Leishman cross to give the Reds the lead and a second from Roger Hunt five minutes later completes a 2-0 victory.

13 April 1988

Liverpool take a 3-0 lead against Nottingham Forest at Anfield. Following an intricate move by John Barnes, Ray Houghton and John Aldridge, the latter plays a low cross into the middle of the Forest box, and Gary Gillespie sweeps home a high shot past the keeper from eight yards out.

16 April 2001

Dietmar Hamann picks the ball up inside his own area, before firing a superb 70-yard diagonal pass to Robbie Fowler. The Liverpool striker crosses into the box, and both David Unsworth and Scott Gemmill miss their kicks for Everton and the ball falls to Markus Babbel, who follows up to drive the ball home from 15 yards.

21 November 1998

Vegard Heggem carries the ball towards the Aston Villa box before playing a sideways pass to Robbie Fowler, who takes one touch before dispatching a low shot from 22 yards into the bottom right of the net to put the Reds 3-1 up at Villa Park.

14 January 2006

With both Liverpool and Spurs competing for a Champions League berth behind runaway leaders Chelsea, this is a tight affair at Anfield. What proves to be the only goal of the game arrives just before the hour mark, as Australian forward Harry Kewell watches a cross into the box before meeting the ball on the full and volleying past Paul Robinson for his first goal in more than a year.

30 October 2019

Alex Oxlade-Chamberlain hits a world-class strike against his former club. Trailing 4-2 in the Carabao Cup at home to Arsenal, Oxlade-Chamberlain nips in to steal the ball off an Arsenal defender before unleashing a 22-yard screamer into the top right of the Gunners net to make it 3-4.

10 December 2019

A goal perhaps only Mo Salah could score and, ironically, it is easily the most difficult of several chances the Egyptian has been presented with against Red Bull Salzburg. As a long ball is played out of defence towards Salah, a Salzburg defender gets his head on it, but Salah is first to the loose ball on the corner of the box. The keeper rushes out to challenge, but Salah touches the ball past him and almost out of play on the right, before whipping a shot in from the tightest of angles that squeezes in the far post to score the Reds' second goal in 100 seconds and make it 2-0 on the night.

59

28 April 1976

Trailing 2-0 in the UEFA Cup Final first leg at Anfield, Ray Kennedy runs on to an inviting short pass from Steve Heighway, and strikes a superb left-foot shot from 20 yards into the top right-hand corner to halve the deficit against Club Bruges.

16 March 1977

Having conceded a precious away goal, Liverpool need two goals to get past St Etienne in the European Cup third round second leg. Just before the hour mark, a cross from the right finds John Toshack, who cushions a pass off his thigh to Ray Kennedy, who drills the ball home from 12 yards to make it 2-1.

15 October 1994

Having led through Robbie Fowler's first-half goal, Blackburn Rovers score twice in five minutes to edge 2-1 ahead in the Premier League fixture at Ewood Park. But just two minutes after falling behind, Liverpool equalise in spectacular fashion, as John Barnes acrobatically volleys home from inside the Rovers box to make it 2-2.

25 May 2005

Liverpool's remarkable recovery is complete when, just before the hour mark, Gennaro Gattuso pulls down Steven Gerrard in the area as he is poised to equalise.

Dida saves Xabi Alonso's spot kick, but the Spanish midfielder follows up to score the rebound with Milan's defenders looking on in stunned disbelief, after seeing the score go from 3-0 in their favour to 3-3 in less than six minutes.

27 September 2008

In a tight Merseyside derby at Goodison Park, Robbie Keane breaks free in the Everton box, before whipping a cross into the middle for Fernando Torres to volley home the opening goal of the game.

60

9 February 1901

Tommy Robertson becomes the first Liverpool player to be sent off during a 2-0 defeat in the FA Cup against Notts County.

18 April 1964

Party time at Anfield with only an hour played, as Liverpool score a third goal in the space of seven minutes to seal the title against Arsenal. Gordon Milne – and the irrepressible Peter Thompson – are involved to lay the ball on for Roger Hunt, who strikes another long-range effort past Furnell to make it 5-0 overall and seal a sixth top-flight title for the Reds.

17 August 1964

Liverpool secure victory even with 30 minutes of their first ever game in the European Cup remaining. Gordon Wallace gets his second of the game on the hour, heading home an Ian Callaghan cross to make it 4-0 to the Reds in the preliminary round first-leg tie away to Icelandic minnows Knattspyrnufélag Reykjavíkur.

15 November 1969

Bobby Graham rises to meet a superb Emlyn Hughes cross from the right to put Liverpool 2-0 up against West Ham United at Anfield. The game, covered by *Match of the Day*, is the first to be shown on the programme in colour rather than black and white.

10 August 1974

In one of the most infamous moments in Wembley history, Kevin Keegan and Billy Bremner exchange blows during the 1974 FA Charity Shield clash with Leeds United. The bad blood has flowed between the teams for a few years but, for such a sanguine fixture, this is something that hasn't really been seen before. Referee Bob Matthewson has no option other than to send both players off, in a game that Liverpool eventually win 6-5 on penalties after a 0-0 draw.

14 October 1978

Liverpool increase their lead to 3-0 against Derby County. A long ball from defence is headed on by David Johnson and into the path of Kenny Dalglish, who controls it, deftly shakes off his marker, and then chips the ball over the keeper as he comes off his line to meet him.

14 May 1988

Liverpool, trailing 1-0 to Wimbledon in the FA Cup Final at Wembley, are awarded a penalty. John Aldridge steps up but sees his spot kick saved by Dave Beasant – the first ever missed in an FA Cup Final – and the 'Crazy Gang' go on to win the game in one of the FA Cup's biggest shocks ever.

31 March 2007

Fabio Aurelio's second superb assist of the game sees Liverpool go 3-0 up against Arsenal on the hour mark. Aurelio whips in a free kick from the left of the Gunners box, and Daniel Agger gets just enough of his head on the ball to send it into the far corner of the net.

3 February 2002

Steven Gerrard's sumptuous through-ball to Emile Heskey – played from his own half with the outside of his right boot – puts the Reds' striker clean through against Leeds United. There's still plenty to do as he approaches Nigel Martyn, but the England man knocks it around the keeper before slotting home from a tight angle to put Liverpool 2-0 up at Elland Road.

26 February 2012

Trailing 1-0 to Cardiff City at Wembley in the 2012 League Cup Final, Liverpool finally level on the hour mark, as Andy Carroll's header is glanced on by Luis Suarez, but the Uruguayan's effort hits the post and Martin Skrtel is quickest to react, prodding the ball home from close range to make it 1-1.

6 November 2016

Liverpool hit five in an hour with a nicely worked goal against Watford. Jordan Henderson plays an incisive pass through the Hornets defence and into the path of Roberto Firmino, who holds the ball up inside the box before playing a short ball across to Sadio Mané, who nips in between two dozing defenders to make it 5-0.

14 January 2018

Bobby Firmino puts the Reds back in front with a superb individual goal. Chasing a pass towards the Manchester

City goal, he shoulder-charges John Stones off the ball, before dinking a shot over Ederson and in off the far post to make it 2-1 in an Anfield thriller.

61

23 November 1946

Jack Balmer draws Liverpool level against Arsenal at Anfield. The Gunners, second from bottom in the First Division, have stunned the league leaders with two goals in two minutes towards the end of the first half, cancelling Balmer's earlier penalty out, but the Reds' skipper makes it 2-2, and in doing so, edges closer to managing a hat-trick of hat-tricks in successive games.

19 April 1966

A game that helps Liverpool fans fall in love with European football – Tommy Smith scores to put the Reds 1-0 up against Celtic in the European Cup Winners' Cup semi-final second leg at Anfield. Having lost the first leg at Parkhead by a single goal, Bill Shankly's men go looking for the second goal that will book their first European final. Smith's 25-yard free kick skips through the crowded, muddy Celtic box and into the bottom corner of the net to set up a rousing finale.

10 May 1973

Kevin Keegan, having scored twice already and seen a penalty saved, sends in a deep corner into the Borussia Mönchengladbach box where it is met by the head of Larry Lloyd, who powers the ball past the keeper to put the Reds 3-0 up in the first leg of the 1973 UEFA Cup Final at Anfield.

28 April 1976

Just two minutes after pulling a goal back in the UEFA Cup Final first leg against Club Bruges at Anfield, Liverpool level the score after a superb sweeping move ends with Kevin Keegan spinning off his marker and crossing it low into the box, where Ray Kennedy hits a low shot past the keeper but on to the post – the lurking Jimmy Case toe-pokes the ball over the line to send the Kop wild.

1 January 2007

The Reds are labouring to break down Sam Allardyce's physical and committed Bolton Wanderers at Anfield. The visitors have already beaten Liverpool once this season, and with two thirds of this game gone, look set for a point at least, but as a cross comes in from the right, Peter Crouch, with his back to goal, strikes an acrobatic volley that gives Jussi Jääskeläinen no chance, to finally break the deadlock.

8 May 2012

Chelsea keeper Ross Turnbull completes a miserable evening at Anfield by gifting Liverpool a fourth goal. Turnbull's casual clearance from the left of his box goes straight to Jonjo Shelvey, who immediately fires a powerful half-volley into the roof of the net from 30 yards out with the goal unguarded to make it 4-1 to the Reds.

20 April 2016

Liverpool punish Everton again as Lucas finds himself in acres of space before threading a ball into the box, where

Daniel Sturridge makes no mistake with a low left-foot drive past Joel Robles to make it 3-0 for the Reds.

1 January 2018

Another Sadio Mané stunner. Drawing 0-0 against Burnley at Turf Moor, Liverpool press for the opening goal – and Mané doesn't disappoint. Trent Alexander-Arnold fires in a low pass from the right, and Mané seems to take the ball off Alex Oxlade-Chamberlain – but he swivels around to strike an unstoppable rising shot past Nick Pope from 20 yards to put the Reds in front.

62

3 April 1974

Liverpool regain the lead against Leicester City in the FA Cup semi-final replay at Villa Park. The Reds have gone ahead just after the break through Brian Hall, only for the Foxes to level within two minutes, but this stunning strike puts Bill Shankly's men on their way to victory. John Toshack plays a lofted pass into Kevin Keegan's path, and the diminutive striker takes the shot first time on the volley and the ball sails over Peter Shilton into the top right-hand corner for a quite brilliant goal.

10 May 1986

Liverpool take the lead in the 1986 FA Cup Final with a second goal in the space of six minutes, as Ian Rush finds Jan Mølby in the Everton box, and the Reds' Danish playmaker slots a low cross to the far post for Craig Johnstone to prod home and make it 2-1.

3 February 2002

Emile Heskey gets his second goal in two minutes as Liverpool go 3-0 up against Leeds United at Elland Road. After a corner ball causes a scramble in the Leeds box, the ball falls to Heskey, who spins to fire the ball into the roof of the net.

27 September 2008

Having already put Liverpool 1-0 up at Goodison Park, just three minutes later, Fernando Torres doubles his and the Reds' lead. Robbie Keane finds Dirk Kuyt but the ball bobbles loose to Torres, who makes no mistake from eight yards.

14 January 2018

Liverpool make it two goals in two minutes against champions-elect Manchester City at Anfield. With the Reds tearing City's defence apart at will, Mo Salah finds Sadio Mané on the edge of the box, and after controlling the pass, the Senegalese striker looks up before lashing a rising left-foot shot into the left-hand corner of Ederson's net to make it 3-1 against the unbeaten Blues.

24 April 2018

Liverpool look to have sealed a place in the Champions League Final with barely an hour played of the semi-final first leg against AS Roma. Already coasting home, Mo Salah drops a shoulder and plays a low cross to Roberto Firmino in the six-yard box, and the Brazilian taps home to make it 4-0. It means Salah has scored two and made two against his former club.

30 October 2019

Having trailed 4-2, Liverpool storm back to make it 4-4 against Arsenal in the Carabao Cup. The ball is played to Divock Origi on the edge of the Gunners box, and the Belgian striker does a Cruyff turn before unleashing a powerful right-foot shot from 18 yards to put the Reds on level terms in a breathless game against the North London side.

63

11 August 1979

Liverpool double their lead against Arsenal in the FA Charity Shield at Wembley. The move that leads to the goal begins with a superb charge out of defence from Alan Hansen, who threads a pass to Kenny Dalglish – the Reds talisman superbly turns his marker inside the box, before coolly curling a right-foot shot past Pat Jennings in the Arsenal goal.

20 August 1988

John Aldridge scores his second of the game as Liverpool come from behind to beat Wimbledon 2-1 in the FA Charity Shield at Wembley. It is Aldridge's second of the game and proves to be the winner against the feisty Dons.

28 April 1990

Despite Steve Nicol appearing to be tripped outside the box, the referee awards a penalty as Liverpool close in on the title against QPR at Anfield. John Barnes converts the spot kick to put the Reds 2-1 up, and with title challengers Aston Villa drawing 3-3, the goal proves to be decisive in the title race, with Liverpool claiming a record 18th championship.

23 March 1991

First Division leaders Liverpool continue to punish bottom side Derby County at the Baseball Ground. Steve Nicol wins possession midway inside the Rams half, before playing a short pass to John Barnes, who plays a one-two with Ray Houghton, before playing a pass to his left, where Nicol is on hand to finish the move he started with a powerful left-foot shot that makes it 6-1 for the Reds.

16 April 2005

Trailing 2-1 to Tottenham at Anfield, the Reds get back on level terms with a surprisingly excellent volley from Sami Hyypia. Steven Gerrard has missed the chance to equalise from the spot just five minutes earlier, when a high clearance is watched all the way by Hyypia, who then volleys a low shot home from 20 yards.

1 January 2007

Just like buses, you wait for one and then two come along in quick succession. The Reds have finally broken Bolton Wanderers' disciplined rearguard when Peter Crouch opens the scoring just past the hour, and two minutes later Steven Gerrard doubles the advantage with a stunning volley. Picked out by Dirk Kuyt's pinpoint cross, the Reds captain still has plenty to do with two defenders lurking, but he gets there first and sends an unstoppable shot past Jussi Jääskeläinen from eight yards out to make it 2-0.

23 January 2016

Bobby Firmino gets his second of the game, as Liverpool come from 3-1 down at Carrow Road to make it 3-3. Adam Lallana's low cross in from the left finds the Reds striker in the box, and he calmly slots the ball home from eight yards out.

5 May 2016

Liverpool get a vital second goal against Villarreal that puts Jürgen Klopp's men ahead on aggregate in the Europa League semi-final. Roberto Firmino sets the first goal up after seven minutes, and the Brazilian's superb skill and vision sets up the second as he collects the ball on the edge of the box before calmly putting Daniel Sturridge clear in the box, and the striker tucks away a low shot just inside the left-hand post, to make it 2-0 on the night and 2-1 on aggregate.

14 August 2016

A quite brilliant goal from a very talented player. As Sadio Mané takes the ball down the right flank, there seems little danger for Arsenal, but he drives towards the box before moving past one challenge, cutting inside another, and then curling a powerful left-foot shot past Petr Cech to make it 4-1 for the Reds against the Gunners at the Emirates – not a bad way to mark your debut!

64

8 December 1962

Roger Hunt puts Liverpool 2-0 up at Sheffield Wednesday. The Reds are already leading through Kevin Lewis's first-half strike, but Hunt's effort seals victory for Bill Shankly's side, and is also the club's 4,000th goal in all competitions.

25 May 1977

Steve Heighway claims his second assist of the 1977 European Cup Final, as his arrowed corner is met with a thumping Tommy Smith header to give the Reds a 2-1 lead over Borussia Mönchengladbach in Rome.

10 May 1978

Liverpool take on Club Bruges in the 1978 European Cup Final at Wembley. With the majority of the 92,500 fans behind them, the Reds try to break down the stubborn Belgians, but it isn't until the introduction of sub Steve Heighway that things start to happen for Bob Paisley's men. The winger begins to stretch the Bruges defence and only moments after his arrival, the breakthrough comes. Under pressure, Graeme Souness manages to control the ball, play an angled pass to Kenny Dalglish in the box, and the brilliant Scot dinks a deft chip over the diving Birger Jensen to send much of Wembley wild with delight. It proves to be the only goal of the game.

2 September 1978

Liverpool go 6-0 up against Tottenham at Anfield with more than 25 minutes still to play. The least memorable of the six goals scored to that point, Phil Neal drives a penalty into the top-left corner of the net, as the visitors' miserable afternoon continues.

14 May 1995

Liverpool level against Kenny Dalglish's Blackburn Rovers at Anfield. England winger John Barnes calmly strokes home a left-wing cross to make it 1-1 in a game where Rovers need a win to guarantee the Premier League title.

14 March 1998

In a thrilling game at White Hart Lane, Paul Ince scores a spectacular overhead kick to make it 2-2 against Spurs. In a topsy-turvy game, Ince's acrobatic effort brings the Reds level and the game ends 3-3.

19 April 2003

Having been pegged back at 1-1 at Goodison Park, Danny Murphy hits one of the best goals of his career, and scores the final goal of the Merseyside derby to seal victory for the Reds. Collecting a loose ball 30 yards out, Murphy tees up a shot before curling a sumptuous strike into the top right-hand corner of the Everton net.

5 May 2012

Sub Andy Carroll pulls a goal back for Liverpool in the FA Cup Final against Chelsea at Wembley. Having only come on nine minutes earlier, Carroll makes an immediate impact as the ball falls to him in the box, and after turning John Terry this way then that, he fires a powerful shot high into the roof of the net to make it 1-2 – though it won't be enough for Kenny Dalglish's men, with no further goals scored in the game.

65

28 April 1976

Kevin Keegan makes it three goals in six minutes as he makes no mistake from the penalty spot to put the Reds 3-2 up in the 1976 UEFA Cup Final first leg. Steve Heighway is pulled down (probably inches outside the box), but the ref awards the spot kick to complete a remarkable turnaround and end the scoring in the opening leg.

11 August 1979

Terry McDermott scores his second of the game and Liverpool's second goal in three minutes, as the Reds go 3-0 up in the FA Charity Shield against Arsenal. A lovely move with David Johnson and Kenny Dalglish involved sees the latter spot McDermott's charge into the box with a short pass, and the Reds midfielder pokes a low shot under Pat Jennings to all but seal victory for Bob Paisley's talented side.

26 November 1989

A stunning John Barnes free kick from 20 yards out puts the Reds 2-0 up against Arsenal. The England winger fires a left-foot, curling effort with plenty of power and pace over the Gunners wall and into the top right-hand corner to double the Reds' advantage.

6 March 2011

Dirk Kuyt puts a massive dent in Manchester United's Premier League title hopes as he completes a well-earned hat-trick. Maxi Rodriguez fires in a free kick from 25 yards, but Edwin van der Sar spills the ball, and Kuyt is first to react as United go on to suffer only their third loss in 29 games.

27 September 2014

With the score still 0-0, Liverpool win a free kick 25 yards from the Everton goal. Of course, there's only one man to take the set piece, and Steven Gerrard doesn't disappoint as he hits a shot over the wall and into the net, with Toffees keeper Tim Howard only able to palm the shot into the roof of the net.

17 April 2019

Liverpool go 2-0 up in the Stadium of Light against Porto, and 4-0 up on aggregate, to all but guarantee a place in the Champions League semi-final. Trent Alexander-Arnold is the architect as he plays a low pass into the path of Mo Salah, who finishes confidently with a left-foot shot from just outside the box.

66

21 November 1998

In a thrilling game at Villa Park, Robbie Fowler completes his hat-trick to repel the hosts' spirited fightback. Leading 3-2, the ball finds its way to Jamie Redknapp, who crosses in from the left of the Aston Villa box towards Robbie Fowler who, despite the attention of two defenders and the goalkeeper, brings the ball down before gently volleying in from five yards to seal a 4-2 win.

14 April 2016

Though 3-1 down to Borussia Dortmund at Anfield and 4-2 down on aggregate, Liverpool keep battling on, and when Philippe Coutinho and James Milner exchange passes, the move ends with the Brazilian firing a low shot past the keeper from the edge of the box to keep the Europa League quarter-final tie alive.

67

19 April 1966

Geoff Strong rises to meet Ian Callaghan's superb cross from the right flank and power his header past the Celtic keeper to put Liverpool 2-0 up against Celtic at Anfield. Strong, playing through the pain barrier with a nasty injury, ploughs on, and his header is testament to his bravery and determination to get the Reds over the line in the European Cup Winners' Cup semi-final second leg. With no further scoring, it confirms Liverpool's first of many European finals, with a date against Borussia Dortmund at Hampden Park in the final.

12 September 1989

John Aldridge becomes the first Liverpool player to come on as a sub and immediately take a penalty, against Crystal Palace. Aldridge scores to make it 6-0 in what will be his final appearance for the Reds before joining Real Sociedad.

19 August 2000

Bradford City have managed to frustrate the Reds and midway through the second half, the Bantams are still level at 0-0. But Emile Heskey is about to change everything when he picks up the ball just outside the box, drifts past one defender before hitting a powerful, angled shot past the keeper from ten yards out, for what is the only goal of the game and to the delight of the Anfield crowd.

68

23 November 1946

Jack Balmer scores his and Liverpool's third to make it three hat-tricks in three consecutive matches – a club record. Balmer's third against Arsenal means he becomes only the third player to achieve this most unique feat, and the cheers of the 51,000-plus Anfield crowd can probably be heard all the way back to North London. The Reds go on to win 4-2 – and no, Balmer didn't get the fourth ...

5 May 1966

Roger Hunt puts Liverpool level in the European Cup Winners' Cup Final against Borussia Dortmund at Hampden Park. The Reds have gone behind to the German side just seven minutes before, but Peter Thompson's superb run down the right wing and subsequent low cross finds Hunt, who powers home a shot from ten yards into the roof of the Dortmund net. The German side, with justification, are incensed as Thompson seems to have run the ball out of play before crossing, but the referee waves away appeals and awards the goal.

9 May 1992

Dean Saunders drives towards the Sunderland goal, before passing to Michael Thomas on the edge of the Sunderland box – the former Arsenal midfielder takes it past one defender but stumbles, and the ball rolls into the path of Ian Rush, who rolls a low shot past keeper Tony

Norman to put Graeme Souness's side 2-0 up in the 1992 FA Cup Final.

2 April 1995

For the second time in the 1995 League Cup Final, Steve McManaman picks up the ball and attacks the Bolton Wanderers defence, dancing past the full-back before cutting inside, drifting past another challenge, and placing a low shot past Keith Branagan to put the Reds 2-0 up at Wembley and on their way to more League Cup glory.

14 January 2018

Liverpool complete eight minutes of sublime attacking football with a third goal in a whirlwind spell against Manchester City. With City on the ropes and clinging on, Ederson rushes out to clear the ball outside of his box, but his clearance is poor and collected by Mo Salah, who controls the ball and then, from 40 yards, sends a chip sailing over the Brazilian keeper to make it 4-1 and send Anfield berserk.

69

30 April 1966

Liverpool have been pegged back to 1-1 against Chelsea, in a game that Bill Shankly's men know victory will mean they are First Division champions ahead of second-placed Burnley. Roger Hunt has given the Reds the lead just after half-time, and it is Hunt who scores what proves to be the winner. Hunt goes past one challenge, then weaves right, then left, before hitting a low drive that Chelsea keeper John Dunn stops but watches in horror as the momentum of the shot sees the ball roll over the line to make it 2-1. For Dunn, credited by many with the Reds' first goal, it caps a miserable day.

5 December 1999

A memorable moment as Steven Gerrard scores the first of his 186 Liverpool goals. It's clear the teenager has a special talent as he attacks the Sheffield Wednesday defence, drifting past one challenge, before a shimmy leaves another defender on his backside, and then sliding a low shot past the keeper to put the Reds 3-1 up. Definitely an 'I was there' moment!

24 April 2018

It's all too easy for the Reds as Roberto Firmino climbs highest to nod a James Milner corner into the bottom left of Alisson Becker's net to make it 5-0 against a poor AS Roma side. It completes the Reds' scoring in the first leg, and although the Italians look dead and buried, they will score two late goals to open up a glimmer of hope for the second leg.

13 March 2019

With the game delicately balanced at 1-1 away to Bayern Munich, Liverpool score a crucial second goal. Simplicity itself, James Milner's deep corner meets the head of Virgil van Dijk, who powers the ball down and past Manuel Neuer to put the Reds in control of the Champions League round of 16 second leg.

2 October 2019

Relief at Anfield as Mo Salah restores Liverpool's lead. Red Bull Salzburg have come from 3-0 down to make it 3-3, with three goals in 21 minutes, but Fabinho's interception outside the Austrians' box is nodded down by Roberto Firmino into the path of Salah, who controls the ball before prodding home from eight yards out to make it 4-3, with what will be the winning goal of a thrilling contest.

70

5 October 1993

Robbie Fowler completes an unforgettable night with his fifth of the game against Fulham. Nigel Clough threads a superb ball that dissects the Cottagers defence and runs into the path of Fowler, and the teenager finishes by lifting his shot over the diving keeper to make it 5-0 for Liverpool and emphatically dump Fulham out of the League Cup.

15 March 2006

Fernando Morientes scores his first Liverpool goal to seal a healthy victory over Fulham. Luis Garcia whips in a cross from the right flank, and Morientes leaps to head the ball past the keeper and into the net from ten yards to make it 3-1 for the Reds.

9 May 2011

Having scored in the first and seventh minutes in a blistering start at Craven Cottage, Maxi Rodriguez completes his second hat-trick in three Premier League matches, as he picks the ball up midway inside the Fulham half, before deciding to have a crack at goal and sending an unstoppable shot past the keeper from 25 yards out.

4 November 2017

Liverpool go 4-1 up against West Ham United at the London Stadium. Sadio Mané brings the ball forward before spotting Mo Salah free on the left of the Hammers box – he lofts a pass to the Egyptian, who controls the pass before firing a precise low shot just inside the right-hand post and past Joe Hart to complete a fine win for Jürgen Klopp's side.

71

28 August 1971

A stunning header by John Toshack puts Liverpool ahead in an entertaining battle with Leicester City at Anfield. Both sides have seen leads wiped out in the space of a minute in the first half, as the teams go into the break at 2-2. But it is the Reds who have the final say, as Emlyn Hughes cuts inside of a challenge on the edge of the box, before firing a shot towards goal that Toshack dives and heads past Peter Shilton to make it 3-2.

6 November 1982

Ian Rush becomes the first player to score a hat-trick in a Merseyside derby for 47 years, as he puts Liverpool 4-0 up at Goodison Park. The move starts in defence, before Kenny Dalglish picks up possession in his own half and plays a defence-splitting pass that sets Rush clear, and although his first shot strikes the foot of the post, he is first to the rebound to complete his treble and end the game as a contest.

23 February 2002

Nicolas Anelka scores his first Liverpool goal to earn the Reds a point in the Merseyside derby. After a stuttering performance that has seen Everton take a second-half lead, a moment of quality as Michael Owen's pass is dummied by Emile Heskey, allowing Danny Murphy to play Anelka in and the French striker scores with ease to make it 1-1.

72

21 April 2009

Fernando Torres brings Liverpool level for the second time against Arsenal at Anfield. Albert Riera spots Torres on the edge of the Arsenal box, before delivering a low cross that the Spaniard controls, turns and fires home into the bottom right corner to make it 3-3 in a thrilling Premier League encounter.

73

21 April 1923

Liverpool make it back-to-back title triumphs, as Harry Chambers levels to make it 1-1 against Huddersfield Town at a packed Anfield. With nearest challengers Sunderland failing to win, it leaves the Reds five points clear with only two games remaining. It is the club's fourth top-tier title.

16 May 2001

Having seen a 3-1 lead pegged back by Alavés in a thrilling UEFA Cup Final in Dortmund, Liverpool regain the lead through Robbie Fowler. Gary McAllister spots Fowler's run inside from the left flank, plays a pass into his path, and the Reds legend does the rest, drifting past two challenges before hitting a crisp right-foot drive into the bottom corner from 15 yards out to make it 4-3.

3 February 2013

Steven Gerrard thumps home a spectacular 30-yard-plus shot to put Liverpool 2-1 up against Manchester City at the Etihad. The defending Premier League champions have earlier taken the lead, but Gerrard's superb strike makes it 2-1 to the Reds in a game that will end 2-2.

10 March 2016

Roberto Firmino scores a crucial second goal as Liverpool take on Manchester United in the Europa League round of 16 first leg. Adam Lallana gets to the corner of the six-yard box before playing a short pass to Firmino, who fires into the top corner from seven yards out to make it 2-0.

16 December 2018

Looking to go top of the Premier League, Liverpool are being held 1-1 by Manchester United when Xherdan Shaqiri enters the fray off the bench. Sadio Mané tricks his way past one United defender on the left, before crossing low into the six-yard box. David de Gea pushes the ball clear, but only as far as Shaqiri, who lashes a shot in off the underside of the crossbar to make it 2-1 for the Reds.

74

4 May 1974

Steve Heighway races on to John Toshack's clever header to sweep the ball past Newcastle United goalkeeper Liam McFaul and put the Reds 2-0 up in the 1974 FA Cup Final.

6 May 1997

Teenager Michael Owen becomes Liverpool's youngest ever goalscorer aged 17 years and 144 days old, when he scores just 16 minutes after coming off the bench. However, it proves too little, too late, with Wimbledon already 2-0 up. The Reds go on to lose 2-1, and in doing so, all but hand the Premier League title to Manchester United – four points ahead – with two games remaining.

18 December 1999

Titi Camara receives a throw-in on the left of the Coventry City box, and controls the ball with one foot before spinning and firing a 25-yard volley into the top right-hand corner to give the Reds a 2-0 lead in the Premier League clash at Anfield.

23 October 2004

Liverpool are leading 1-0 against Charlton Athletic, when Luis Garcia picks up the ball more than 30 yards from goal, and with little else on, he tries his luck with a curling piledriver that sails into the top right-hand corner to make it 2-0.

25 January 2012

Craig Bellamy scores the goal that sends Liverpool to a first Wembley final in 16 years. Having won the first leg of the Capital One Cup semi-final against Manchester City at the Etihad Stadium, the Reds find themselves 2-1 down at Anfield, until a well-worked equaliser puts Liverpool back in front on aggregate. Dirk Kuyt cuts in from the right before passing the ball to Bellamy, who exchanges passes with Glen Johnson before firing a low shot past former City team-mate Joe Hart, to make it 2-2 and 3-2 on aggregate.

23 January 2016

Liverpool recover from 3-1 down to take a 4-3 lead away to Norwich City. The Canaries defence implodes when a blind back-pass is intercepted by James Milner who, with just the keeper to beat, feigns one shot and then drills the ball home as cool as you like to put the Reds in the box seat at Carrow Road.

75

4 May 1965

Tommy Smith's clever flick finds Roger Hunt in behind the Inter Milan defence, and the striker fires a shot that is saved but bundled home by Ian St John to put the Reds 3-1 up in the European Cup semi-final at Anfield.

21 August 1971

Kevin Keegan pulls a goal back against Newcastle United at St James' Park. The Reds, trailing 3-1 thanks to a hat-trick from debut boy Malcolm Macdonald, win a corner on the left, and Peter Thompson's inswinging cross is scrambled home by Keegan, but it won't be enough to save Liverpool from defeat.

7 November 1981

Ian Rush puts Liverpool 3-0 up in the Merseyside derby at Anfield – but he doesn't know much about it! A break down the right flank by Terry McDermott sees the midfielder play a pass into Kenny Dalglish, who in turn finds David Johnson in space on the right of the Everton box – he hits a shot that Jim Arnold does well to beat out, but as a defender attempts to clear the danger, the ball hits Johnson before deflecting in off Rush to seal the victory for the Reds.

26 March 1983

Alan Kennedy pulls Liverpool level with a long-range left-foot shot against Manchester United in the 1983 League Cup Final. The Reds have trailed to Norman Whiteside's early effort as they look to win the trophy for a record third successive time at Wembley.

17 April 1993

Coventry City have thrashed Liverpool 5-1 at Highfield Road earlier in the season and the Reds are keen to avenge their heaviest defeat to the Sky Blues. Thankfully, Mark Walters has his shooting boots on, and has already scored a hat-trick by the time David Burrows pops up with a rare goal – a sweet left-foot sizzler from 25 yards – to make it 4-0 on the day.

29 September 2007

With Wigan Athletic holding the Reds at the JJB Stadium, one moment of magic finally swings the game Liverpool's way, as Israeli playmaker Yossi Benayoun spins off his marker, before turning another defender inside out and rolling the ball past the keeper for what proves to be the winning goal.

15 December 2013

Liverpool, having lost the previous six matches away to Tottenham, go 3-0 up at White Hart Lane. Jordan Henderson's run takes him wide of the Spurs box, and his cross is deflected into the path of Luis Suarez, who, from the right, chips the ball into the middle, where Jon Flanagan connects beautifully on the half-volley to send a powerful shot in off the underside of the crossbar.

1 March 2015

Title-chasing Manchester City's record at Anfield has been poor to say the least over the years, but with only 15 minutes left, they are holding Liverpool 1-1 and perhaps hopeful of nicking a late winner. Then, Raheem Sterling carries the ball towards the City box before finding Philippe Coutinho, who cuts inside and strikes a sweet, curling effort up and over Joe Hart to make it 2-1 and seal another Reds win over the Mancunians.

20 April 2016

Philippe Coutinho completes Everton's misery, as he puts the Reds 4-0 up at Anfield in the Merseyside derby at an ecstatic Anfield. Joe Allen spots the Brazilian on the edge of the box and plays a low pass to the left, where Coutinho immediately skips past one challenge, before curling a low shot into the bottom right-hand corner, giving Joel Robles no chance.

27 October 2019

Liverpool go 2-1 up in a tense clash with Tottenham. Serge Aurier's attempt at a clearance only catches the back of Sadio Mané's leg in the box, and referee Anthony Taylor awards a penalty kick. Mo Salah dispatches the ball past Gazzaniga with a low shot that the Spurs keeper barely even moves for.

76

31 January 1981

Leicester City's Jim Melrose scores what will prove to be the winning goal against Liverpool at Anfield. The Foxes striker completes a comeback for the visitors, but the shock win ends an 85-match unbeaten home run for the Reds, which lasts one week shy of three years, during which there are 69 home wins, 16 draws and no defeats – Liverpool score 212 goals during that run and concede just 35. Incredible.

4 May 1976

Liverpool travel to face Wolves at Molineux knowing that a draw will ensure a ninth First Division title. QPR, in pole position, can only watch and hope Wolves pull off a shock win, with their season complete and them sitting top by a point. QPR's inferior goal average means a point will be enough for Bob Paisley's men, but Wolves still have a sniff of escaping relegation if they can win and other results go their way. The hosts go ahead after 13 minutes, and a crowd of almost 50,000 – including thousands from Merseyside – can hardly watch as the clock steadily ticks down. Then, finally, the Reds equalise. Ian Callaghan plays a short pass to Tommy Smith, who swings a cross into the box, and John Toshack glances the ball into the six-yard box where Kevin Keegan nips in ahead of the keeper to send the travelling masses wild.

2 September 1978

Liverpool score their final – but best – goal of the afternoon against Tottenham. A quite magnificent sweeping move sees David Johnson ping a pass out towards Steve Heighway on the left flank, and his first-time cross is met with a thumping header from Terry McDermott to make it 7-0. Scintillating football from a quite brilliant Liverpool team.

24 November 2018

A resolute Watford have held out until the 67th minute, before Liverpool's dominance finally starts to pay off. Having gone ahead through Mo Salah, the Reds are awarded a free kick around 22 yards from goal – Trent Alexander-Arnold steps up to curl a shot past Ben Foster to all but seal the points against the Hornets.

19 January 2019

Liverpool take the lead against Crystal Palace for the first time in an exciting Premier League clash at Anfield, as James Milner manages to cross the ball in from the right, and after keeper Julian Speroni makes a terrible hash of an attempt to clear the danger, the ball drops on the goal line, where Mo Salah finishes off the job for his 50th Premier League goal for the Reds and makes it 3-2 in the process.

30 November 2019

Alisson Becker is shown the red card as he handles the ball outside of his box against Brighton at Anfield. The referee has no option other than to show the Brazilian a straight red after he prevents Leandro Trossard from taking the ball past him. Though the Seagulls score from the resulting free kick, the Reds hold on to win 2-1, and move 11 points clear of defending champions Manchester City.

77

16 April 1977

Kevin Keegan gets the all-important second goal for title-chasing Liverpool against Arsenal at Anfield. David Johnson cuts in from the right before unleashing a low shot that is saved by Jimmy Rimmer, but Keegan lashes the loose ball home with a low drive from 12 yards to make it 2-0.

14 March 2009

In a game Liverpool can't afford to lose, Fabio Aurelio puts the Reds 3-1 up at Old Trafford. United, who could go ten points clear of Liverpool with ten games remaining, have gone ahead on 23 minutes through Cristiano Ronaldo, before conceding twice before the break. Awarded a free kick 25 yards from goal, Aurelio strikes a curling free kick over the wall with such pace that Edwin van der Sar doesn't even move.

26 October 2013

After Luis Suarez has scored a hat-trick to put Liverpool 3-0 up against West Brom, it is Daniel Sturridge's turn to take centre stage. He collects a cushioned header from Steven Gerrard, before heading towards the West Brom box. As he gets to 20 yards from goal, he sends a delightful left-footed chip over the keeper and into the net to make it 4-0 for the Reds.

29 November 2017

Sadio Mané torments Stoke City's Ryan Shawcross on the right before getting to the byline and clipping a cross towards the back post, where Mo Salah blasts a left-foot volley into the back of the net from close range to double the Reds advantage at the Britannia Stadium.

8 December 2018

Mo Salah completes his hat-trick away to Bournemouth with a goal all of his own doing. After skipping past one defender, he draws the Cherries keeper off his line before taking it around him – then, as the keeper makes a second attempt, Salah sells him a dummy that leaves the Egyptian with two defenders to beat on the line – which, of course, he does with ease to make it 4-0 at the Vitality Stadium.

10 April 2018

Liverpool seal a place in the Champions League semi-final after Roberto Firmino capitalises on a Manchester City mistake to run into the area, before calmly placing the ball past Ederson to make it 2-1 to the Reds in the second leg at the Etihad, and 5-1 to Liverpool overall.

17 April 2019

Game, set and match at the Stadium of Light, as Liverpool go 3-1 up against Porto. Jordan Henderson picks out the run of Roberto Firmino, and delivers a superb cross with pace, so that Firmino needs only the slightest of headers to send the ball past the keeper.

78

17 April 1922

Liverpool are crowned champions for the first time in 16 years with a 2-1 win over title challengers and defending champions Burnley at Anfield. Dick Forshaw restores the Reds' lead with just 12 minutes remaining to set up the scenario needed to win the league. Liverpool are aware that victory over the Clarets and a defeat for second-placed Tottenham will mean the Reds cannot be caught – and despite a fraught last few minutes, the stars align, and Liverpool, with three games remaining, cannot be caught. It's the Reds third top-tier title in total.

14 October 1978

A difficult goal is made to look simplicity itself, as Steve Heighway plays a low pass into the path of Kenny Dalglish in the Derby County box, and the Scot, in turn, spots a clever run by Ray Kennedy and plays the ball into his path, and Kennedy makes no mistake to put the Reds 4-0 up at Anfield.

4 January 1994

Neil Ruddock completes a remarkable Liverpool comeback at Anfield. Having trailed 3-0 after just 23 minutes, two Nigel Clough goals put the Reds back in touching distance of Sir Alex Ferguson's side, and when sub Stig Inge Bjørnbye's cross is whipped into the United box with just 12 minutes remaining, it is the burly Neil Ruddock who meets the ball with a firm header to make it 3-3.

14 April 2016

In a breathtaking Europa League quarter-final tie at Anfield, Mamadou Sakho equalises for the Reds to make it 3-3 with Borussia Dortmund. As a corner comes in, Sakho bravely stoops to head home and put Liverpool within one goal of a thrilling comeback.

79

13 April 1988

Peter Beardsley caps a mesmeric performance by scoring Liverpool's fourth against Nottingham Forest. The diminutive playmaker has been pulling the strings throughout the game with a stunning display, but he has to wait until 11 minutes from time to get on the scoresheet, and he owes the goal to team-mate John Barnes, who nutmegs one defender on the left, before gliding past another and pulling the ball back for Beardsley, who fires a low right-foot shot into the bottom corner of the net.

13 April 1991

John Barnes caps a wonderful performance as he races on to Ian Rush's clever flick and clear of the Leeds United defence, before clipping a low shot past John Lukic to end the home fans' hopes of a comeback and put the Reds 5-2 up at Elland Road, in a thrilling First Division game Liverpool eventually win 5-4.

30 August 2003

Leading 2-0 at Goodison Park, Michael Owen nips in ahead of goalkeeper Steve Simonsen before crossing into the six-yard box. The ball is headed clear but only as far as Harry Kewell, who instinctively hits the ball on the half-volley straight into the middle of the unguarded net to make it 3-0 for the Reds.

20 September 2006

A breathtaking goal few at Anfield will ever forget from Xabi Alonso. Leading 1-0 against Newcastle United, Alonso wins back possession midway inside his own half. He immediately looks for options to start a counter-attack, but after pushing the ball forward a couple of yards, he spots Magpies keeper Steve Harper off his line and so hits the ball high and with power from 60 yards, and as Harper realises he needs to rush backwards, he slips, and the ball sails into the back of his net. A quite spectacular goal.

7 May 2019

Trent Alexander-Arnold wins a corner off Sergi Roberto, and, thinking on his feet, spots Divock Origi in the middle of the penalty area, takes the corner quickly, and finds the striker completely unmarked to sweep home from close range and put the Reds 4-0 up against Barcelona in the second leg of the Champions League semi-final at Anfield. It also puts Liverpool 4-3 up on aggregate on the night – a lead that won't be surrendered in what is regarded as perhaps the greatest Champions League comeback of all time.

1 June 2019

Divock Origi doubles Liverpool's lead with an excellent finish to all but secure victory in the 2019 Champions League Final.

Tottenham fail to clear the ball after Virgil van Dijk's blocked attempt, and Jöel Matip's intelligent pass finds Origi unmarked to the left of the area. The Belgian striker fires a left-footed attempt under the dive of Hugo Lloris and into the corner of the net to make it 2-0 for the Reds.

80

16 April 1906

Jack Parkinson scores his second goal in six minutes, as Liverpool attempt an unlikely comeback against Bolton Wanderers at Burnden Park. Knowing victory could hand the Reds – who have led the First Division since mid-December – their second top-flight title triumph, a nervy Liverpool find themselves 3-1 down with 75 minutes played. The hosts hold on to win the game, but good news soon filters through that nearest challengers Preston have lost 2-0 at Sunderland, meaning, with just two games remaining, the Reds – five points ahead – cannot be caught.

14 October 1978

Liverpool round off a fantastic performance with a fifth goal against Derby County at Anfield. Steve Heighway finds David Johnson on the halfway line, and he immediately plays a clever ball into the path of Alan Hansen who is driving towards goal. With Anfield willing Hansen to score, he instead passes to his right, where Kenny Dalglish has the simplest of tasks to roll the ball home with the Rams keeper stranded.

1 November 1999

Vegard Heggem has only been on the pitch two minutes when he scores the best goal of his Liverpool career. The Norwegian right-back bursts past one challenge on the edge of the box and drives on, somehow eluding three Bradford City challenges, before slotting a low shot into the bottom corner to put the Reds 3-1 up at Anfield.

19 May 2001

Michael Owen rounds off the scoring as Liverpool beat Charlton Athletic 4-0 at The Valley. The victory confirms the Reds have qualified for the Champions League qualifying stage for the first time since the competition changed from the European Cup in 1992.

8 December 2004

With time seemingly running out on Liverpool's Champions League campaign, a second sub finds the net after just coming on. Still needing to win by two goals, the Reds finally edge ahead after a goalmouth scramble sees Neil Mellor slide home from six yards to make it 2-1 against Olympiacos with ten minutes still remaining ...

13 August 2006

Liverpool snatch what proves to be the winning goal in the 2006 FA Community Shield clash with Chelsea. With the scores level at 1-1, Craig Bellamy, making his Reds debut, races down the flank, before delivering the perfect cross for Peter Crouch to head home and ensure the perfect start to the 2006/07 campaign.

16 December 2018

Liverpool finally get the breathing space needed after a tricky encounter with Manchester United at Anfield. Mo Salah finds Roberto Firmino, who flicks the ball back towards the Egyptian – but Shaqiri arrives first to curl a left-foot shot past David de Gea from the edge of the box and put the Reds 3-1 up.

27 February 2019

Liverpool go 4-0 up against Watford at Anfield thanks to a Virgil van Dijk header. Trent Alexander-Arnold's dangerous free kick picks out the Dutchman's head, and he powers the ball past Ben Foster from close range.

5 April 2019

The title-chasing Reds are under a period of sustained pressure from Southampton at St Mary's. The Saints have earlier led before Naby Keita levels, but the hosts are looking for a second to further damage Liverpool's chances of winning the Premier League. But a rapier-like counter-attack sees Mo Salah race towards goal, before sending a cleverly improvised left-foot shot past Angus Gunn to make it 2-1.

81

14 January 1981

Visits to Manchester City's Maine Road usually end in comfortable victories for Liverpool during the late 1970s and 1980s. The League Cup semi-final first leg, however, proves a much tighter affair, with the hosts holding firm and having what appears to be a perfectly good goal disallowed, before Terry McDermott's free kick finds Ray Kennedy's run, and the Reds midfielder expertly slots home from close range to give Liverpool a slender but vital advantage to take back to Anfield.

16 September 1990

With Liverpool already 3-0 up in the First Division clash with Manchester United at Anfield, Ray Houghton spots Peter Beardsley's run and lofts a ball over the United defence, and Beardsley calmly lifts his shot over the onrushing Les Sealey to complete his hat-trick and a 4-0 rout for the Reds.

14 April 2009

Lucas Leiva scores from distance to give the Reds late hope at Stamford Bridge. Liverpool have led 2-0 against Chelsea and have levelled the aggregate score to 3-3 – but Chelsea have stormed back to 3-3 on the night and 6-3 on aggregate. Lucas's deflected strike makes it 6-4 on aggregate.

21 November 2015

A deep Adam Lallana corner drops kindly for Martin Skrtel, who lashes a right-foot howitzer into the top right of the Manchester City net to make it 4-1 for Liverpool at the Etihad, and complete a resounding win for Jürgen Klopp's side.

5 May 2016

Roberto Firmino caps a superb performance by having a huge role in Liverpool's third and decisive goal against Villarreal. The Brazilian has assisted the first two goals against the Yellow Submarine, and it is his run and low cross that results in the third, as his pass finds Daniel Sturridge who mishits his shot, and Adam Lallana flicks the ball into the net from close range to make it 3-0 on the night and 3-1 on aggregate, as the Reds close in on the Europa League Final.

29 November 2016

A memorable day for teenager Ben Woodburn, as he breaks Michael Owen's record to become Liverpool's youngest ever goalscorer, as he bags the second goal in a 2-0 victory over Leeds United. Woodburn is aged just 17 years and 45 days at the time.

12 May 2019

Sadio Mané rises to glance home Trent Alexander-Arnold's cross for his second of the game and to put Liverpool 2-0 up against Wolves. But with Manchester City winning 4-1 at Brighton, there is to be no Premier League title party at Anfield, although with a Champions League Final still to come, there is nothing but pride in how Jürgen Klopp's side have performed during 2018/19, and, on any other occasion, 97 points would easily be enough.

82

25 May 1977

After Kevin Keegan is fouled in the Borussia Mönchengladbach penalty area, Phil Neal calmly steps forward to slot home the penalty that puts the Reds 3-1 up, and seals a first European Cup success for the club.

25 March 1978

Kenny Dalglish seals a 3-1 win against struggling Wolves at Molineux. The goal is Liverpool's 5,000th in all competitions, and keeps the Reds' slim title hopes alive.

27 May 1981

Liverpool win the European Cup for the third time in five years, as Terry McDermott's throw-in is collected by a barnstorming Alan Kennedy, who bursts into the box before hitting a rising angled shot past Real Madrid keeper Agustín Rodríguez for the only goal of the game at the Parc des Princes in Paris.

3 April 1999

In a see-saw Merseyside derby at Anfield, Patrik Berger seals victory for the Reds. Everton have gone ahead in the first minute, before Liverpool strike back with two goals in six minutes to lead at the break. But in a tense finish, a corner is cleared to the edge of the Everton box, where Berger volleys a low drive into the bottom corner to seal the points.

9 September 2000

Having led 2-0 against Manchester City at Anfield, Liverpool are pegged back to 2-2 with 81 minutes played. But the Reds restore their lead immediately as a cross into the box is cleared by City defender Steve Howey, but only as far as Dietmar Hamann, who chests the ball and then volleys past Nicky Weaver from 20 yards out for a spectacular winning goal.

26 August 2005

Pepe Reina launches a huge goal kick, which Luis Garcia expertly chests into the path of Djibril Cisse and, after defender Sergei Ignashevich's attempt at a clearance strikes the Reds striker and loops over the keeper's head, Cisse is left with an empty net to tap home, as Liverpool draw level in the 2005 UEFA Super Cup Final against CSKA Moscow.

31 March 2007

Peter Crouch completes a memorable day as he restores Liverpool's three-goal cushion against Arsenal at Anfield by scoring his third of the afternoon. Jermaine Pennant's cross is touched on by Dirk Kuyt and collected by Crouch, who brings the ball down with a deft touch, nudges it to the side of the Arsenal defender, before drilling home from close range to make it 4-1 and help the Reds leapfrog the North Londoners into third spot in the Premier League.

25 February 2009

Liverpool secure a famous win at the Bernabéu with a late winner in the round of 16 first leg against Real Madrid.

Awarded a free kick on the right of the Real box, Fabio Aurelio whips in a free kick, and Yossi Benayoun manages to rise among a crowd of players and head powerfully past Iker Casillas to secure a 1-0 lead to take back to Anfield.

28 April 2012

The Reds are already leading 2-0 against Norwich City at Carrow Road when Elliott Ward loses the ball on the halfway line to Luis Suarez (scorer of both goals). The Uruguayan looks up, spots Canaries keeper John Ruddy off his line, and hits a 45-yard shot that sails over Ruddy and into the net to complete his hat-trick with a quite superb goal.

83

15 January 1959

Geoff Twentyman scores from the penalty spot as Liverpool pull a goal back against non-League Worcester City in the FA Cup third round tie at St George's Lane, but the home side holds firm for a famous 2-1 win and completes one of the FA Cup's biggest shocks of all time.

10 May 1986

Liverpool all but wrap up the 1986 Merseyside derby FA Cup Final, as Ronnie Whelan bursts forward before spotting Ian Rush free in the box. The Republic of Ireland midfielder stops before lofting a pass to Rush, who controls and then fires home to make it 3-1 against Everton.

6 November 1991

Mark Walters sends Anfield wild as he makes it 3-0 against Auxerre in the UEFA Cup second round second leg tie. Having trailed 2-0 from the first leg, few have given the Reds any hope of progressing in the competition, but Walters collects Jan Mølby's pass, before skipping past a couple of challenges and driving a low shot past the keeper to send Liverpool into the next round.

12 May 2001

Markus Babel manages to knock down a free kick into the box, and Michael Owen swivels and thumps the ball past goalkeeper David Seaman to make it 1-1 in the 2001 FA Cup Final against Arsenal.

14 April 2009

Liverpool go 4-3 ahead at Stamford Bridge and threaten one of the most incredible Champions League comebacks of all time. Albert Riera gets around the Chelsea full-back and whips in a cross that Dirk Kuyt heads home from close range to put the Reds within a goal of a stunning second leg victory. With the aggregate scores at 6-5 in Chelsea's favour, a fifth goal would see Liverpool progress to the semi-final – but Chelsea go on to score again, and the game ends 4-4 and 7-5 overall.

12 September 2015

A quite magnificent goal that unfortunately comes too late to save Liverpool from defeat at Old Trafford. Manchester United are already 2-0 up when Jordan Ibe dinks in a cross from the right that is only half-cleared by the United defence, and the ball falls to Christian Benteke, who acrobatically volleys a scissor-kick shot that rockets past David de Gea to half the deficit – but United go on to win 3-1.

27 February 2019

Virgil van Dijk scores his second goal in the space of three minutes, with another excellent assist from a Liverpool wing-back. This time, it is Andy Robertson's inch-perfect cross that finds van Dijk's head, and he once again makes no mistake from close range to make it 5-0 over Watford at Anfield.

84

4 May 1968

Liverpool produce a late smash and grab at Elland Road to keep hopes of winning the title alive, but severely damage Leeds United's. Leeds are leading 1-0 and will move within a point of joint leaders Manchester City and Manchester United with a victory – plus Don Revie's men have a game in hand with just two games remaining. But Leeds, unbeaten at home all season, can't clear a goalmouth scramble, and Chris Lawler bundles the ball home from close range to silence the home support and make it 1-1. But there is more drama to come 60 seconds later ...

16 March 1977

Needing one more goal to send the Reds into the European Cup semi-final, Liverpool's super sub does it again to make it 3-1 against St Etienne. Chasing a punt forward, Fairclough gets to the ball ahead of three defenders as he approaches the box. He calmly gets the ball under control and tucks a low shot past the keeper from ten yards to almost lift the Kop's roof off and complete one of the most memorable European nights Anfield has ever seen.

3 April 1993

The only bright spot on a miserable day at Ewood Park, an instinctive Ian Rush goal gives the Liverpool fans who haven't left the ground early scant consolation. Trailing 4-0 to Blackburn Rovers, a clearance drops on the edge of the Rovers box, and Rush spins to volley a powerful shot from 18 yards to reduce the deficit to 4-1.

22 January 2002

Liverpool stun Old Trafford with a goal six minutes from time that settles the game and puts the Reds within two points of the summit. Steven Gerrard is the architect as he picks up the ball midway inside the United half, before curling a sumptuous pass into the path of Danny Murphy, who times his run to perfection before gently lifting the ball over Fabien Barthez to make it 1-0.

25 March 2006

Harry Kewell scores a spectacular third Liverpool goal to finally give the Reds breathing space in a fraught Merseyside derby at Anfield. Having lost Steven Gerrard to a red card after only 18 minutes, Liverpool have scored either side of the break to lead 2-0, until Tim Cahill halves the deficit. As the clock ticks down, the ball falls to Kewell 25 yards out, and his left-foot swerving shot flies like a rocket into the top corner to seal the game for the ten-man Reds.

15 December 2013

Luis Suarez is at his impish best as he puts the Reds 4-0 up away to Spurs. Luis Alberto, having just replaced Lucas five minutes earlier, receives the ball midway inside the Tottenham half, and plays it into the path of Suarez, and as Hugo Lloris races off his line, the Uruguayan lifts his shot up and over the keeper and into the net for a quite brilliant goal.

16 March 2014

Luis Suarez completes a comprehensive victory for Liverpool against Manchester United at Old Trafford. Daniel Sturridge scuffs a shot that Suarez, just onside, stops and then places past David de Gea to put the Reds 3-0 up.

13 March 2019

Liverpool book a place in the Champions League quarter-finals, as Mo Salah spots Sadio Mané's run towards the six-yard box, before sending in a cross that Mané heads past Manuel Neuer, to make it 3-1 at the Allianz Arena and 3-1 on aggregate.

17 April 2019

Liverpool complete a rout at the Stadium of Light with a set-piece goal. James Milner's corner is glanced on by Sadio Mané, and Virgil van Dijk thumps a header from six yards out, as the Reds go 4-1 up against Porto and 6-1 on aggregate in the Champions League quarter-final second leg.

85

4 May 1968

Liverpool score a second goal in a minute to destroy Leeds United's hopes of winning the title. Chris Lawler has just levelled for the Reds, and he is initially credited with the second Liverpool goal 60 seconds later, but it is a Bobby Graham bullet header from the edge of the box that does the damage – although Lawler is just a few feet away from connecting himself – that somehow squeezes over the line to give the Reds a dramatic 2-1 win. Though both sides can still win the league, the big winners are Manchester City, who are crowned champions a week later.

23 April 1973

Anfield erupts as Kevin Keegan scores the goal that seals an eighth top-tier title. Already 1-0 up and with time running out for Leeds United, a cross from the byline is dropped by the keeper as he tangles up with one of his own defenders, and Keegan nips in to take the ball away and then rifle a shot into the roof of the net from eight yards to double the lead. Though it is mathematically possible that Arsenal could finish above Liverpool, the game is recognised as confirmation of an eighth top-division title for Bill Shankly's side.

4 May 1976

Having levelled on 76 minutes against Wolves, the Reds are on track to win the title on goal average from QPR. But when Phil Neal's cross eventually falls to John Toshack, the Welshman holds the ball, twists this way and that with his back to goal, before turning and firing the ball under the keeper to make it 2-1 and all but seal a ninth First Division title.

6 November 1982

Ian Rush completes an unforgettable day for himself and for Liverpool, as he scores the Reds' fifth at Goodison Park. Sammy Lee drives out from defence before playing a superb pass into Rush's path, and the Welsh legend calmly moves the ball around Neville Southall before slotting into the empty net to score his fourth of the game and Liverpool's fifth.

25 April 1984

Ronnie Whelan picks up the ball on the left, beats the full-back, and whips a cross into the Dinamo Bucharest box, where a defender attempts to head the ball clear from no higher than a foot off the ground – the ball gets stuck underneath him, and Ian Rush nips in to nudge it a few inches to the left, before rifling a low shot into the bottom corner to put the Reds 2-1 up and all but guarantee a place in the European Cup Final.

86

14 August 1965

David Herd's goal for Manchester United on 81 minutes looks to have clinched the FA Charity Shield clash with Liverpool at Old Trafford – but with time running out, Ron Yeats levels for Bill Shankly's talented side to claim a 2-2 draw and ensure the Shield is shared for that season.

3 April 1974

John Toshack seals Liverpool's place in the 1974 FA Cup Final with a smart low finish four minutes from time. Leading 2-1 against Leicester City in the semi-final replay at Villa Park, Peter Cormack plays the ball behind a tiring Foxes defence, and Toshack, with just Peter Shilton to beat, takes his time before calmly stroking a shot under the keeper to make it 3-1.

6 December 1977

David Fairclough scores Liverpool's fifth of the night against Hamburg in the European Super Cup. Jimmy Case plays a one-two with Terry McDermott, before whipping a cross in from the right that Fairclough leaps to head home from close range.

12 November 2000

Emile Heskey seals an easy 4-1 win over Coventry City at Anfield with a sumptuous goal. Heskey, having scored his first of the game five minutes earlier, chests the ball down on the edge of the box, before volleying a delightful chip over Chris Kirkland with the outside of his right boot to end the contest.

2 March 2003

With Manchester United pressing for a late equaliser, Liverpool clear the ball to the halfway line, where Dietmar Hamann eventually collects and breaks forward before sliding a pass to Michael Owen, who drills a low shot past Fabien Barthez to seal a 2-0 League Cup Final triumph for the Reds.

8 December 2004

Steven Gerrard sends Anfield wild as he scores the goal that sends the Reds into the Champions League round of 16. Despite going behind in the first half, Liverpool completely turn the game on its head with two goals from subs making it 2-1, and then a howitzer of a third from Gerrard. It is the sort of goal only Stevie G seems to score, as Jamie Carragher's chip is nodded down by Neil Mellor, and Gerrard thumps a half-volley past the keeper from 20 yards to make it 3-1 against Olympiacos.

28 October 2014

Mario Balotelli scores his first goal for Liverpool as he rises to head home Fabio Borini's cross to make it 1-1 with Swansea City in the League Cup tie at Anfield. The Reds have fallen behind to the Swans and look to be on their way out of the competition, before the Italian's equaliser.

9 August 2015

With just four minutes left of a hard-fought opening day tussle with Stoke City at the Britannia Stadium, Philippe Coutinho receives the ball before rolling his marker midway into the Stoke half, then hitting a superb shot into the top right-hand corner of the Potters net from 30 yards out to give the Reds a 1-0 victory.

87

13 March 1982

Ronnie Whelan sweeps home a late equaliser from David Johnson's low cross, as Liverpool rescue the 1982 League Cup Final from the jaws of defeat. Trailing by an early goal against Spurs at Wembley, the leveller sets up extra time.

16 August 1986

In an all-Merseyside FA Charity Shield clash at Wembley, Ian Rush equalises to secure a 1-1 draw with Everton, and ensure the Shield is shared and spends six months either side of Stanley Park.

11 May 2002

Nicolas Anelka rounds off a 5-0 win over Ipswich Town at Anfield. The victory gives the Reds their highest Premier League finish up to that point.

20 November 2011

Glen Johnson scores a brilliant individual goal against his former club Chelsea to silence Stamford Bridge. The Liverpool right-back controls a pass, then cuts effortlessly past Ashely Cole into the box, has too much pace for another defender's challenge, before placing the ball past Petr Cech to make it 2-1 and seal the points for the Reds.

12 January 2014

In a thrilling match at the Britannia Stadium, Daniel Sturridge finally seals three points for the Reds after some innovative trickery. Leading 4-3 in a match that ebbs and flows, Luis Suarez's cross finds Sturridge at the far post, and the Reds sub sees his volley pushed out by Jack Butland. Sturridge keeps the ball in play by first chesting it, then heading it, before volleying another low shot that beats the keeper and seals a 5-3 win.

2 November 2019

Trailing 1-0 away to Aston Villa with only three minutes of normal time remaining, Sadio Mané picks the ball up on the right and spots Andy Robertson's run into the box, delivers a superb cross, and the Scottish left-back powers a header past Tom Heaton to level the scores.

88

17 August 1964

Roger Hunt wraps up Liverpool's first European match with a powerful shot from 20 yards, making it 5-0 for the Reds away to Icelandic minnows Knattspyrnufélag Reykjavíkur in the European Cup preliminary round first leg.

4 May 1974

Tommy Smith claims his second assist of the 1974 FA Cup Final, after a fine team move ends with Smith crossing into the box for Kevin Keegan to score his second of the game and secure a 3-0 win over Newcastle United at Wembley.

17 September 1974

Ray Kennedy completes Liverpool's biggest ever win, as he strokes home the Reds' final goal against Strømsgodset. The Norwegian side are totally overwhelmed at Anfield, and Kennedy's goal is the third in the space of three relentless minutes from Billy Shankly's men, who show their opponents the ultimate respect by playing at full throttle. There are nine different scorers, including Phil Thompson's first two goals for the club, as the European Cup Winners' Cup first round first leg ends 11-0 to Liverpool.

6 December 1977

Kenny Dalglish completes a rout over Hamburg in the second leg of the European Super Cup at Anfield. Already

5-0 up, Dalglish is first to react when David Johnson's shot from close range is saved, with the former Celtic star making no mistake from six yards out. The 6-0 loss means the Reds win 7-1 on aggregate – not the homecoming Kevin Keegan has perhaps imagined.

13 April 1988

Liverpool complete a 5-0 rout of Nottingham Forest with a goal just before full time. Made by Nigel Spackman, who wins the ball midway inside the Forest half before exchanging passes with Peter Beardsley, it is John Aldridge who bags his second of the game, turning Spackman's low cross home from close range.

12 May 2001

Chasing a long ball towards the Arsenal box, Michael Owen muscles his way between two Arsenal defenders, before hitting a low left-foot shot past David Seaman to score his second goal in five minutes, to make it 2-1 to the Reds and effectively seal the 2001 FA Cup Final at the Millennium Stadium in Cardiff.

89

2 September 1893

Joe McQue seals a 2-0 win for Liverpool in the Reds' first ever league game. The victory comes at the aptly named Paradise Field against Middlesbrough Ironopolis – Malcolm McVean has earlier scored the club's first ever official goal.

4 May 1976

A beautiful goal. Leading 2-1 and just seconds from being confirmed as First Division champions, Kevin Keegan plays the ball to the feet of Ray Kennedy in the Wolves box, and the elegant midfielder slips past his marker before rifling the ball into the roof of the net with an angled shot from his sweet left foot. Cue pitch invasion!

3 February 2002

Michael Owen rounds off a fantastic day for the Reds, as he makes it 4-0 away to Leeds United. A long throw into the box is headed on by Emile Heskey, and Owen then heads on to the crossbar, before reacting fastest to prod the rebound home in front of the travelling hordes from Merseyside. The win puts Liverpool within two points of the Premier League summit.

23 May 2007

Dirk Kuyt pulls a goal back against AC Milan in the 2007 Champions League Final, but the Reds, now trailing 2-1 to the Italians, run out of time in their quest to win Europe's premier club competition yet again. Daniel Agger flicks on Jermaine Pennant's corner, and Kuyt nods home, but it's too little, too late.

10 March 2009

The icing on the cake as Andrea Dossena scores Liverpool's fourth of the night against Real Madrid. Javier Mascherano's low cross from the right finds the Italian defender inside the box, and his low shot is parried by Iker Casillas – but only into the opposite corner of his net, as Madrid's misery is complete. The 4-0 win means the Spanish giants lose 5-0 on aggregate.

23 November 2013

In a see-saw Merseyside derby at Goodison Park, Liverpool have twice lost the lead and fallen 3-2 down, after two goals from Romelu Lukaku give the Toffees the advantage. But when a free kick is awarded on the right of the Everton box, Steven Gerrard whips in a free kick that Daniel Sturridge glances home to claim a last-gasp point for the Reds.

15 December 2013

The icing on the cake as Liverpool complete a 5-0 rout of Tottenham at White Hart Lane. Luis Alberto wins the ball and plays a short pass to Luis Suarez, who in turn slips Raheem Sterling in, and the young winger makes no mistake from eight yards with a low shot past Hugo Lloris. It is Tottenham's worst home defeat in 16 years.

29 September 2018

Chelsea look set for three points thanks to Eden Hazard's 25th-minute goal at Stamford Bridge, and as sub and former Chelsea striker Daniel Sturridge – who has only replaced James Milner three minutes earlier – receives the ball, there seems little on, so he decides to have a crack at goal from 20 yards out and strike a beautiful, curling left-foot drive with power that gives Kepa no chance, and earns the Reds a vital last-minute point.

90

17 November 1973

Kevin Keegan completes his hat-trick in the dying embers of an entertaining clash with Ipswich Town at Anfield. Leading 3-2, the superb Steve Heighway is felled in the box by Geoff Hammond, who has endured a torrid 90 minutes against the Reds winger. The referee awards a penalty, and Keegan emphatically dispatches the spot kick into the top left-hand corner to complete a 4-2 win and a fine individual performance.

12 September 1989

Steve Nicol completes what he starts by making it 9-0 for Liverpool against Crystal Palace. Nicol's seventh-minute goal starts the rout, and as David Burrows bursts into the box and slides a cross into the six-yard box, it's Nicol who is there to drill a low shot past the keeper to send the Reds top of the First Division.

23 March 1991

Ray Houghton's last-minute effort sees Liverpool equal the club record away victory, as the Reds go 7-1 up at Derby County. The seventh strike is also the pick of the bunch, as Peter Beardsley plays a short corner to Houghton who spots John Barnes on the left of the Rams box – Houghton plays a short pass to feet, Barnes makes a delightful back-flick that puts Houghton clear, and the Republic of Ireland international tucks the ball past Peter Shilton to complete a memorable day for the league leaders.

20 March 1993

Anfield goes crazy as Ronnie Rosenthal scores a last-minute winner in the 148th Merseyside derby. With the score 0-0 and just seconds remaining, Ian Rush loses the attention of three defenders before playing a superb reverse pass to substitute Rosenthal, who has made an intelligent run into the box, and the Israeli drills a low shot that gives Neville Southall no chance and wins the game 1-0 for the Reds.

3 November 1998

The gloss of a dramatic away goals triumph over Valencia is tarnished, as Liverpool see two players sent off for a last-minute flare-up. The Reds have managed to all but secure a 2-2 draw with the La Liga side in the UEFA Cup second round second leg at the Mestalla, when Valencia player Amadeo Carboni appears to strike Steve McManaman, who retaliates – Paul Ince tries to prevent things getting any worse and all three players are shown the red card.

5 February 2000

Sub Danny Murphy ends any hopes of a Leeds United comeback at Anfield with a stunning goal. Liverpool have led 2-0, but the visitors have halved the deficit and are looking for a late equaliser, until Murphy sends a shot into the top right-hand corner of the net from 25 yards to give the keeper no chance and complete a 3-1 victory.

13 January 2016

Having twice led earlier in the game, Liverpool trail 3-2 to Arsenal after an Olivier Giroud double. There is last-minute drama to come, however, as Jordan Henderson's cross into the box finds the head of Christian Benteke, and the Belgian nods the ball back across into the path of Joe Allen, who drives the ball into the bottom left corner to make it 3-3 – a fitting way to end a thrilling game.

18 September 2018

Liverpool, having led 2-0 but pegged back to 2-2 by Paris Saint-Germain, have the final say with an excellent last-gasp winner. Virgil van Dijk comes forward with the ball, before playing to his right for Roberto Firmino. The Brazilian takes on one defender, dummies a shot, before shifting it on to his right foot and firing a low shot into the bottom left corner to send Anfield wild.

31 March 2019

Liverpool grab a last-gasp winner against Tottenham at Anfield. Having just survived a two-on-one break by the visitors, the Reds get the goal that seals three crucial points, as Mo Salah rises to meet a cross into the box from the left, and his header towards goal hits the shins of Toby Alderweireld and gently rolls past Hugo Lloris to send Anfield wild.

4 December 2019

Liverpool seal three points as Georginio Wijnaldum scores the Reds' fifth of a memorable Anfield Merseyside derby. Substitute Roberto Firmino is the creator, as he cuts in from the left before bamboozling a defender and pulling the ball back for Wijnaldum, who fires a low shot across the keeper and into the far right-hand corner of the Toffees net to make it 5-2.

90+1

13 May 2006

Steven Gerrard scores his second of the game to rescue the FA Cup Final and send the game with West Ham United into extra time, as he unleashes a howitzer of a shot from fully 35 yards to send the Liverpool fans wild and tie the game at 3-3.

14 April 2016

With Borussia Dortmund set to go into the Europa League semi-final on away goals, Liverpool, roared on by the Kop, summon up one last attack. Daniel Sturridge cleverly holds up the ball before slipping a pass into the box for James Milner, who gets to the byline before standing a cross up towards the back post for Dejan Lovren to head home a dramatic winner and complete one of Anfield's greatest comebacks ever.

6 November 2016

Georginio Wijnaldum completes a memorable afternoon at Anfield with his first Premier League goal for the Reds. At the heart of the move is Daniel Sturridge, who begins an attack that ends with his low shot from the edge of the box that is saved by the Watford keeper, but only into the path of Wijnaldum, who taps home from close range to make it 6-1.

4 February 2018

With the score at 1-1 and the Reds pressing for a winner. Trent Alexander-Arnold finds Mo Salah, whose cross seems to hit a Tottenham defender's hand – the Egyptian appeals, but then races on to the loose ball, drifts past one challenge before leaving another two defenders for dead with a drop of the shoulder, and then lifts the ball over Hugo Lloris for what seems to be the winner – only for the visitors to snatch an even later equaliser.

92

8 May 1971

Steve Heighway gives Liverpool the lead in the second minute of extra time in the FA Cup Final against Arsenal. The Reds winger collects the ball on the left, and as he edges towards the box hits a low shot that beats keeper Bob Wilson on his near post to put Liverpool 1-0 up at Wembley. The Gunners recover to win 2-1.

90+2

26 May 1989

Drama of the highest calibre at Anfield, but for once, it is in favour of the visitors, not Liverpool. In a thrilling climax to the First Division campaign, Arsenal need to beat the Reds by two clear goals to deny Liverpool an 18th domestic top-flight title. Though 1-0 down, as the game moves into the second minute of added time, it looks as though the Reds have done enough, but as the ball is played through to Michael Thomas, the Arsenal midfielder sees the ball bounce kindly for him as he tries to control it, and Thomas continues into the box before putting the ball past Bruce Grobbelaar to clinch the title for the Gunners.

3 April 1996

Stan Collymore ghosts in on the left side of the Newcastle United box to slam the ball past Pavel Srnicek to give Liverpool a dramatic 4-3 win over Kevin Keegan's side. The Magpies, chasing a first Premier League title, have already led three times before being pegged back by the Reds, but though both sides would settle for a draw, a sweeping move ends with John Barnes and Ian Rush seemingly undecided on what to do as they enter the Newcastle box, until Barnes spots Collymore's run, feeding the ball to the striker, who makes no mistake and sends Anfield crazy in the process.

90+3

16 April 2001

Everton have fought back to 2-2 in the Merseyside derby at Goodison Park, but, deep into added time, Liverpool have one more opportunity. A free kick 35 yards out offers Gary McAllister the chance to whip the ball into the box, but instead the Scotland international goes for goal, catching keeper Paul Gerrard off-guard, and the ball skids off the surface and into the net. Did he mean it? Most certainly!

19 January 2019

Sadio Mané seals three points for the Reds, as he cuts into the Crystal Palace box from the left, before placing an angled low shot into the bottom corner from ten yards to make it 4-2 and give the Reds breathing space in what has been a difficult match.

93

1 May 1965

Despite breaking his collarbone earlier in the game, Gerry Byrne is the Reds hero, as he carries on playing rather than reducing the team to ten men, as no subs were allowed at this time. After Liverpool and Leeds play out a 0-0 draw in the 1965 FA Cup Final, the match moves into extra time, and it is Byrne's cross that is headed home by Roger Hunt to give the Reds the lead.

90+4

14 May 1995

Jamie Redknapp fires a 30-yard free kick into the top left corner of the Blackburn Rovers net to seal a 2-1 win – but Liverpool fans aren't sure whether to laugh or cry! Returning hero Kenny Dalglish is manager of Rovers, who need a win to guarantee winning the Premier League title, and will be pipped if Manchester United better Blackburn's result on the final day. But almost as the ball hits the back of net, news filters through that United have drawn 1-1 with West Ham, and the title is heading to Ewood Park. Anfield celebrates Dalglish's success accordingly.

19 December 2016

In a tightly contested Merseyside derby at Goodison Park, Liverpool snatch a last-gasp winner. Daniel Sturridge cuts in from the right past one challenge, before scuffing a low left-foot shot from 22 yards out. The ball hits the inside of the post, and Sadio Mané is first to react to the loose ball to give Jürgen Klopp's side a 1-0 win.

30 October 2019

Liverpool trail 5-4 in the Carabao Cup against Arsenal and are deep into injury time, when Neco Williams fires in one last-gasp cross from the right into the Arsenal box, and – the man who loves a late goal or two – Divock Origi sends a spectacular scissor kick past the Gunners' keeper to make it 5-5 and send this unforgettable game to penalties.

2 November 2019

Sadio Mané scores a dramatic last-minute winner against Aston Villa. The Reds have trailed up until the 87th minute before Andy Robertson's headed equaliser, but it still looks like two points dropped for Jürgen Klopp's side, until Trent Alexander-Arnold's outswinging corner is expertly glanced at the corner of the six-yard box into the opposite corner of the Villa net to secure a 2-1 win.

90+5

21 April 2009

Yossi Benayoun makes it 4-4 with almost the last kick of the game, as Liverpool snatch a point against the Gunners. Xabi Alonso's deep cross is headed across by Javier Mascherano, nodded on by Ryan Babel, and swept home by Benayoun. It is Liverpool's second successive 4-4 draw, but it is two points dropped in the title race, and hands Manchester United – level on 71 points but with two games in hand – the advantage.

28 October 2014

Dejan Lovren seals a dramatic comeback for the Reds when he nods home an added-time winner against Swansea City in the League Cup. Lovren rises to head Philippe Coutinho's free kick powerfully past the Swans keeper to cap a 2-1 win, despite having been a goal behind with just four minutes of normal time remaining.

23 January 2016

A fittingly dramatic end to a dramatic game. Liverpool have led 1-0, trailed 3-1, led 4-3 and been pegged back to 4-4 in the second minute of added time – breathless stuff, but it isn't quite over.

The Reds go in search of the ninth goal of the game, and in the fifth minute of added time, a frantic goalmouth scramble ends with Adam Lallana firing a half-volley into the ground and into the top right-hand corner of the net to make it 5-4 and win the game against Norwich City at Carrow Road.

5 October 2019

With the 100 per cent start to the 2019/20 season in peril, Sadio Mané is felled in the box by Leicester City's Marc Albrighton deep into added time. Mr Reliable – James Milner – steps up to slot home the penalty and make it eight wins from eight.

95

20 May 1989

Substitute Ian Rush puts Liverpool 2-1 up in extra time in the 1989 FA Cup Final against Everton. Steve Nicol lofts a clever pass to the edge of the six-yard box, where Rush controls before swivelling a high shot past Neville Southall into the roof of the net.

7 January 1998

Liverpool break the deadlock against Newcastle United in a League Cup fifth round tie at St James' Park. The tie has gone into extra time when a fine move involving Paul Ince, Steve McManaman and Robbie Fowler ends with Michael Owen delicately chipping the ball over Magpies keeper Shaka Hislop to make it 1-0 to the Reds.

90+6

2 December 2018

A quite extraordinary finish to the Merseyside derby at Anfield. The Reds have tried in vain to break down Everton's resistance and the game looks set to finish as a goalless draw. With the last throw of the dice and deep into injury time, Trent Alexander-Arnold sends a cross into the Toffees box, but it is cleared to the edge of the box, where Virgil van Dijk balloons a volley high and seemingly out of play. The Dutch defender turns away in disgust at himself, but the ball drops towards the crossbar where Everton keeper Jordan Pickford inexplicably gets a hand to it, effectively keeping the ball in play, and it bounces twice along the crossbar before falling to Divock Origi, who has the easiest opportunity he'll ever have to nod home the winner and send Anfield crazy.

98

26 March 1983

Ronnie Whelan scores what proves to be the winning goal in the 1983 League Cup Final. After attempting a through pass on the edge of the box, the ball comes back to the Republic of Ireland midfielder, who instinctively curls a superb shot into the top right-hand corner to put Liverpool 2-1 up against Manchester United and secure a third successive League Cup triumph.

99

21 December 2019

Liverpool claim their first FIFA World Club Cup with an extra-time winner against Brazilian champions Flamengo in Qatar. With both teams inseparable in normal time and the 90 minutes ending 0-0, Liverpool counter-attack with Jordan Henderson finding Sadio Mané with a fine ball towards the edge of the Flamengo box. Mané controls the pass before laying it to his left where the supporting Roberto Firmino receives the ball in the box before dropping his shoulder to cut back inside – sending a defender and the keeper the wrong way – before hitting a shot into the centre of the net for what will prove the winning goal of the game.

103

7 January 1998

Liverpool double their lead against Newcastle United at St James' Park. Jamie Redknapp's run and pass sees Robbie Fowler fire an angled shot past Shaka Hislop to all but seal the League Cup fifth round tie.

26 August 2005

In extra time in the 2005 UEFA European Super Cup in Monaco, Liverpool take a 2-1 lead. Luis Garcia, afforded acres of space to run into in his own half, makes CSKA pay when he launches a superb 40-yard pass into the path of Djibril Cisse, who with just the keeper to beat, sees his first shot saved, but the rebound falls kindly and he makes no mistake for his second fortuitous strike of the game.

104

20 May 1989

Super sub Ian Rush scores what proves to the winning goal for Liverpool in a thrilling all-Merseyside FA Cup Final at Wembley. John Barnes's cross from the left appears to be just falling short of Rush, but the Welshman cleverly adjusts to stoop and head the ball past Neville Southall and make it 3-2.

107

5 May 1966

Drama in extra time as Liverpool concede what will prove to be the winning goal in the European Cup Winners' Cup Final at Hampden Park. As keeper Tommy Lawrence races off his line to clear a Borussia Dortmund attack, the ball is cleared to the wing, where Reinhard Libuda immediately sends a lofted shot over the stranded Lawrence towards the goal, and as Ron Yeats chases back to clear, the ball hits the underside of the bar before striking Yeat's back and going into the net to put the German side 2-1 up. It is the cruellest of ways to lose the game.

108

26 February 2012

Liverpool finally get their noses in front, as Dirk Kuyt follows up his own blocked shot to put the ball past Cardiff City keeper Tom Heaton and make the score 2-1 to the Reds in the 2012 League Cup Final. The Bluebirds will later level and force a penalty shoot-out that Liverpool win to land the trophy for the eighth time.

109

26 August 2005

Having come from 1-0 down to lead 2-1, Liverpool score a decisive third that seals the UEFA European Super Cup against CSKA Moscow in Monaco. Having scored two goals – both assisted by Luis Garcia – Djibril Cisse returns the favour, as he races down the left flank before picking out the run of Garcia, who heads home from close range to make it 3-1.

111

13 March 1982

Ronnie Whelan scores his second of the 1982 League Cup Final to put the Reds 2-1 up. Kenny Dalglish gets behind the Tottenham defence, and waits for the perfect moment to play the ball across the six-yard box for Whelan to scoop high into the roof of the net from close range.

117

1 May 1965

Ian St John heads home Ian Callaghan's cross to win the FA Cup for Liverpool for the first time. St John's goal puts the Reds 2-1 up against Leeds, and after seeing the final moments out, the famous old trophy heads back to Anfield for the first time in the club's 73-year history.

16 May 2001

A dramatic UEFA Cup Final gets the dramatic end it deserves, as the Reds snatch a late winner against Alavés. The Spaniards have forced extra time after a thrilling 4-4 draw, but then have two players dismissed. Despite the advantage, Liverpool look as though they will be facing penalties, until Gary McAllister's late free kick on the left of the Alavés penalty area sees Delfi Geli glance the cross over his own keeper to seal a 5-4 win in Dortmund.

118

14 March 1981

Alan Kennedy seemingly wins the 1981 League Cup Final at Wembley, as he puts the Reds ahead just two minutes from the end of extra time. But with the Liverpool fans still celebrating, Terry McDermott clears an Alvin Martin header on to the crossbar with his fingertips, and West Ham's Ray Stewart converts the resulting penalty with almost the last kick of the game to force a replay.

119

13 March 1982

Ian Rush ensures Liverpool's 1982 League Cup title defence is a success, as he seals a 3-1 win over Spurs with an extra-time goal just minutes before full time. Sammy Lee's excellent ball out of defence sets Rush away, and the Welsh striker sets up David Johnson, who is initially denied, but then slides the ball across to Rush, who makes no mistake from eight yards out.

Penalty Shoot-Outs

10 August 1974

One of the most bad-tempered FA Charity Shield matches of all time ends 1-1, and Liverpool and Leeds United are forced to decide the result from a penalty shoot-out. The Reds triumph and Bob Paisley's reign starts with a trophy.

Peter Lorimer (Leeds United) – scores 0-1

Alec Lindsay (Liverpool) – scores 1-1

Johnny Giles (Leeds United) – scores 1-2

Emlyn Hughes (Liverpool) – scores 2-2

Eddie Gray (Leeds United) – scores 2-3

Brian Hall (Liverpool) – scores 3-3

Norman Hunter (Leeds United) – scores 3-4

Tommy Smith (Liverpool) – scores 4-4

Trevor Cherry (Leeds United) – scores 4-5

Peter Cormack (Liverpool) – scores 5-5

David Harvey (Leeds United) – misses 5-5

Ian Callaghan (Liverpool) – scores 6-5

Liverpool win 6-5 on penalties.

13 April 1992

Liverpool are held 0-0 by Portsmouth at Villa Park in the FA Cup semi-final. The result leads to a penalty shoot-out.

Martin Kuhl (Portsmouth) – misses 0-0

John Barnes (Liverpool) – scores 1-0

Kit Symons (Portsmouth) – scores 1-1

Ian Rush (Liverpool) – scores 2-1

Warren Neill (Portsmouth) – misses 2-1

Dean Saunders (Liverpool) – scores 3-1

John Beresford (Portsmouth) – misses 3-1

Liverpool win 3-1 on penalties.

25 February 2001

Liverpool edge a tense penalty shoot-out after normal time and extra time fail to separate the Reds and Birmingham City. With Birmingham levelling on 90 minutes to force additional time, many wonder if the Blues are about to win their first League Cup Final for 38 years. However, Liverpool keep their cool in the shoot-out to edge home 5-4 at the Millennium Stadium in Cardiff.

Gary McAllister (Liverpool) – scores 1-0

Martin Grainger (Birmingham City) – misses 1-0

Nick Barmby (Liverpool) – scores 2-0

Darren Purse (Birmingham City) – scores 2-1

Christian Ziege (Liverpool) – scores 3-1

Marcelo (Birmingham City) – scores 3-2

Dietmar Hamann (Liverpool) – misses 3-2

Stan Lazaridis (Birmingham City) – scores 3-3

Robbie Fowler (Liverpool) – scores 4-3

Bryan Hughes (Birmingham City) – scores 4-4

Jamie Carragher (Liverpool) – scores 5-4

Andrew Johnson (Birmingham City) – misses 5-4

Liverpool win 5-4 on penalties.

25 May 2005

Liverpool win the most dramatic Champions League Final of all time after coming back from 3-0 down against AC Milan to draw 3-3, and then secure victory via another equally dramatic penalty shoot-out.

Serginho (Milan) – misses 0-0

Dietmar Hamann (Liverpool) – scores 1-0

Andrea Pirlo (Milan) – misses 1-0

Djibril Cisse (Liverpool) – scores 2-0

Jon Dahl Tomasson (Milan) – scores 2-1

John Arne Riise (Liverpool) – misses 2-1

Kaka (Milan) – scores 2-2

Vladimir Smicer (Liverpool) – scores 3-2

Andriy Shevchenko (Milan) – misses 3-2

Liverpool win 3-2 on penalties.

13 May 2006

After a thrilling 3-3 draw with West Ham United in the FA Cup Final at the Millennium Stadium, the game goes to a penalty shoot-out – and the Reds hold their nerve to win 3-1.

Dietmar Hamann (Liverpool) – scores 1-0

Bobby Zamora (West Ham) – misses 1-0

Sami Hyypia (Liverpool) – misses 1-0

Teddy Sheringham (West Ham) – scores 1-1

Steven Gerrard (Liverpool) – scores 2-1

Paul Konchesky (West Ham) – misses 2-1

John Arne Riise (Liverpool) scores – 3-1

Anton Ferdinand – (West Ham) – misses 3-1

Liverpool win 3-1 on penalties.

26 February 2012

The Reds end a six-year wait for silverware with a League Cup triumph over Cardiff City at Wembley. The game finishes 2-2 after extra time, but Liverpool edge the penalty shoot-out against the Bluebirds – despite missing the first two spot-kicks!

Steven Gerrard (Liverpool) – misses 0-0

Kenny Miller (Cardiff) – misses 0-0

Charlie Adam (Liverpool) – misses 0-0

Don Cowie (Cardiff) – scores 0-1

Dirk Kuyt (Liverpool) – scores 1-1

Rudy Gestede (Cardiff) – misses 1-1

Stuart Downing (Liverpool) – scores 2-1

Peter Whittingham (Cardiff) – scores 2-2

Glen Johnson (Liverpool) – scores 3-2

Anthony Gerrard (Cardiff) – misses 3-2

Liverpool win 3-2 on penalties.

14 August 2019

Liverpool and Chelsea draw 2-2 in the European Super Cup, sending the game to penalties. Sadio Mané levels Olivier Giroud's opening goal, and Mané puts the Reds 2-1 up in extra time, before Jorginho levels from the spot after 101 minutes. The Reds triumph 5-4 in a tense shoot-out.

Roberto Firmino (Liverpool) – scores 1-0

Jorginho (Chelsea) – scores 1-1

Fabinho Tavarez (Liverpool) – scores 2-1

Ross Barkley (Chelsea) – scores 2-2

Divock Origi (Liverpool) – scores 3-2

Mason Mount (Chelsea) – scores 3-3

Trent Alexander-Arnold (Liverpool) – scores 4-3

Emerson Palmieri (Chelsea) – scores 4-4

Mohamed Salah (Liverpool) – scores 5-4

Tammy Abraham (Chelsea) – misses 5-4

Liverpool win 5-4 on penalties.

30 October 2019

Ten goals shared between Liverpool and Arsenal results in the Carabao Cup tie at Anfield going straight to penalties, in a 5-5 draw that probably neither side deserve to lose, but young Reds keeper Caoimhin Kelleher is the toast of Anfield after this shoot-out victory.

> Héctor Bellerin (Arsenal) – scores 0-1
>
> James Milner (Liverpool) – scores 1-1
>
> Matteo Guendouzi (Arsenal) – scores 1-2
>
> Adam Lallana (Liverpool) – scores 2-2
>
> Gabriel Martinelli (Arsenal) – scores 2-3
>
> Rhian Brewster (Liverpool) – scores 3-3
>
> Dani Ceballos (Arsenal) – misses 3-3
>
> Divock Origi (Liverpool) – scores 4-3
>
> Ainsley Maitland-Niles (Arsenal) scores – 4-4
>
> Curtis Jones (Liverpool) – scores 5-4

Liverpool win 5-4 on penalties.

Also available at all good book stores

9781785315466

9781785313929

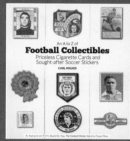

9781785315602

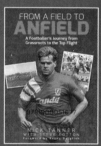

9781785313073

9781785310423

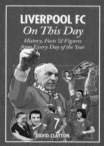

9781908051059

9781908051677

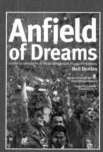

9781905449804

9781785314384